PAPER COLLAGE

THE
SEAGULL
LIBRARY OF
FRENCH
LITERATURE

PAPER COLLAGE

SELECTED APHORISMS AND SHORT PROSE

Georges Perros

Translated by John Taylor

LONDON NEW YORK CALCUTTA

INDIA

This work is published with the support of
Institut français en Inde – Embassy of France in India

Seagull Books, 2021

Originally published in French
Papiers collés 1 © Éditions Gallimard, 1960
Papiers collés 2 © Éditions Gallimard, 1973
Papiers collés 3 © Éditions Gallimard, 1978
Pour ainsi dire © Éditions Finitude, 2004
L'Ardoise magique is included in *Papiers collés 3* © Éditions Gallimard, 1978

First published in English translation by Seagull Books, 2015
Translation and Introduction © John Taylor, 2015

ISBN 978 0 8574 2 843 1

British Cataloguing-in-Publication Data
A catalogue record for this book is available from the British Library

Typeset by Seagull Books, Calcutta, India
Printed and bound by WordsWorth India, New Delhi, India

Contents

Acknowledgements

Many of these aphorisms and short texts were first published, sometimes in different versions, in the following reviews:

International Literary Quarterly 11 (Summer 2010). Available at www.interlitq.org

FragLit 7 (Fall 2010) Available at www.fraglit.com

Michigan Quarterly Review 50(2) (Spring 2011).

The Dirty Goat 25 (Fall 2011).

The Black Herald 2 (Fall 2011).

Plume (Winter 2011–12). Available at http://plume-poetry.com/

The Plume Anthology of Poetry 2012. Edited by Daniel Lawless (Hudson, New Hampshire: Pequod Books, 2012).

Three texts appeared on the 'Writer's Corner' page of the website of the National Endowment for the

Arts (www.nea.gov) when this project won a 2011 translation grant.

Warm thanks to all the editors involved.

The translator would also like to thank Éditions Gallimard and Éditions Finitude for granting us the translation rights to this selection of texts by Georges Perros. May both publishers receive our gratitude for their enthusiasm and helpfulness.

Introduction

Strollers along the coastal heights near Douarnenez, a fishing port located in Brittany at nearly the westernmost point of continental France, come across a signpost summing up the life of Georges Perros and quoting one of his incisive aphorisms. This signpost, braving the Atlantic west winds, offers a fitting memorial for this at once rugged- and tender-hearted writer who remains warmly remembered in France for the touching autobiographical poems collected in *Poèmes bleus* (Blue Poems, 1962) and *Une vie ordinaire* (An Ordinary Life, 1967), for his several volumes of entertaining (or wryly melancholic) letters and, above all, because of *Papiers collés* (Paper Collage, 1960, 1973, 1978), his three volumes of maxims, vignettes, short prose narratives, occasional diary-like notations, critical remarks and personal essays. These three volumes represent par excellence what the French call a *livre de chevet*; that is, a book that can be left for months or years on a bedside table and, every now and then, be dipped into or—more likely—entirely reread.

Georges Poulot (his real name) was born in Paris in 1923. Marked for the rest of his life by the absence of his stillborn twin brother, Perros would later observe in a poem that 'nothing' gave him 'the enviable sensation / of being completely here on the earth'. This existential perspective informs much of what he wrote, while at the same time his writings express affection for daily life and a down-to-earth directness. In this tense ambivalence lies their lasting importance and fascination. Perros constantly raises the question: 'How to live?' In one of his numerous maxims about suicide, the poet wrote: 'There's suicide. That's pretty good. But one should have thought of its opposite.' And in another aphorism: 'The first man who thought of committing suicide humiliated life for all eternity. Life is like someone who remains greatly offended.'

Perros' first loves were the piano, which he studied long enough to become a fine amateur pianist, and the theatre. Initially an actor, he was a member of or consorted with various troupes, including, briefly, the Comédie Française, during the late 1940s and early 50s. But towards the end of this period, during which he had become a close friend of the actor Gérard Philippe as well as the actresses Jeanne Moreau and Maria Casarès, Georges Perros—his pen name alludes

to the Breton village Perros-Guirec—increasingly
turned to literature, first as a reader of manuscripts
for the Théâtre National Populaire, managed by the
well-known stage director Jean Vilar, and then for
Éditions Gallimard. Perros started publishing his
poems, reviews and mini-essays on sundry topics—
often pertaining to the quotidian—in the *Nouvelle
Revue Française* and other literary magazines. He
quipped that he was a *petit noteur* (a little note- or
filler-writer), all the while punning on the homopho-
nous *un auteur* / *un noteur*, but his stylistic freshness
and frank critical judgements were immediately spot-
ted and encouraged by Jean Paulhan, a key Gallimard
editor and luminary. (The engaging *Correspondance
1953-1967* of Perros and Paulhan has been published
by Éditions Claire Paulhan, and it is an enlightening
volume because Perros formulates penetrating insights
into Paulhan's own insufficiently studied *oeuvre*.)
Linked in French literary history (and often in friend-
ship) with the poets and writers—Jacques Réda, Jean
Roudaut, Michel Butor, Jean-Loup Trassard and
others—published by Georges Lambrichs in the 'Le
Chemin' series at Gallimard; and with other writers
—such as the critic Brice Parain or the translator Carl
Gustaf Bjurström—who were likewise associated with
Gallimard, Perros nonetheless lived about as far from
Paris and these friends as is geographically possible.

'Dazzled by the sea', as he admitted, he more or
less permanently settled in Douarnenez towards the

end of 1958. He would later bring his future wife
Tania—who is movingly evoked in several poems—
and her two children to live there with him. Three
more children would be born. For the rest of his
life, Perros lived anonymously in this rather impov-
erished seaside town, scraping a living as a freelance
author and manuscript reader, publishing a few
books, teaching what he called an 'ignorance course'
at the University of Brest (from 1970), corresponding
with his many writer-friends and, whenever he could,
riding his motorcycle along the country roads. In an
early poem, he christens himself 'Georges Machin',
literally, 'George Thingamajig' and suggesting 'John
Doe'. He confesses to a frequent impression of 'not
writing with his own name / and of being here only
by chance.' The image of the fame-shunning, pipe-
smoking, motorcycle-riding poet dwelling far from
the sophisticated capital also belongs to Perros' lasting
reputation which had increased considerably during
the years preceding his death from larynx cancer
in 1978. During these last years of his life, French
poets would make an effort to visit their friend in
Douarnenez. Réda records an encounter in his long
poem 'Escale à Douarnenez', included in *Nouveau
Livre des reconnaissances* (1992):

> Then we went out to down a few glasses of
>   red wine

In the *bistrots* around the port where nearly
>everyone
Hailed you in friendly or timid tones,
And some people, in fact, almost rudely.
But you kept laughing up your sleeve or
>rather in your pipe
And the tough guys at the bar should have
>spared themselves the trouble.
[. . .]
When evening came, we settled in the
>kitchen once again,
Soup, Tania smoking near the stove,
The cat on your knees, the dog between my
>legs,
Your pipe, a big bottle open, your andantino
>voice.
The kids were whooping it up in the
>bedrooms . . .

Although Réda claims that they talked shop only a
little—'What would have been the use?'—he evokes
the man's literary relationship to the appurtenances
of daily life. 'What I listened to as I tasted the
mashed potatoes,' he observes, 'was not separate from
your books. Your fingers / That were dancing above
the oilcloth / Still seemed to be writing down notes
in the air.' Réda puns with the verb *noter* which also
means to write down musical notes. Perros is indeed

admired for his poetic and prose 'music'. As Réda knows (and the same applies to him and his proverbial Vélo-Solex), the legends surrounding Perros, despite their several truths, can somewhat distract the reader of octosyllabic poetry that is subtle in its formal adroitness and use of the colloquial idiom, and of prose that relies on finely shaded puns, multi-layered meanings and, once again, oral syntax. At once colloquial and savant, his style is immediately recognizable.

His sensibility was acute and complex. Behind the folksy, sometimes sighing, sometimes bitter, sometimes sardonic, sometimes resigned voice lurks an intensely sensitive, highly cultivated, introspective and actually quite secretive ruminator on the human condition. His witty misanthropy conceals much affection for friends from all walks of life. In a national literature that has often emphasized autobiographical perspective, Perros' contribution stands out because of his lucid scrutiny both of himself and others (and, specifically, the beloved other, his wife), that is, his simultaneous scepticism about and yearning for love and, especially, lasting friendship. His aphoristic insights into these latter topics are provocative and reveal facets of his deep pessimism, even cynicism, about the possibility of human understanding, as well as his gratitude for times when love and friendship were spawned and subsisted. Writers who knew Perros well still often use the adjective 'fraternal' when recalling him.

In French, the three volumes of *Paper Collage* represent nearly a thousand printed pages of writing. The slightly amusing and semantically complex title is characteristic of the author's puns. *Papiers collés* refers to 'glued bits or scraps of paper' forming a collage, and readers spontaneously think of how the artist Henri Matisse used paper cut-outs to make carefully arranged collages at the end of his life. Moreover, Perros puns on the word *papier* which does not have exactly the same meaning as the English 'paper' (in the sense of an 'academic paper'). Perros alludes to the commissioned book reviews, short prose pieces and personal essays that he wrote for magazines— such prose pieces are still called 'papiers' in literary jargon. The three volumes accordingly gather, in a somewhat puzzling arrangement, short prose writings of several kinds, including maxims that, at times, follow one another down the page and, at other times, offer a single provocative pause between two longer pieces. In the first volume of *Paper Collage*, the author probably reveals his own intentions when he refers to Cubism and observes that 'it would be good if a journal could be written in the same way that Picasso paints. A distorting journal that would show artistry …' I have added to this selection other samples from *Pour ainsi dire* (So to Speak), a book consisting of writings that were rather recently discovered. *Pour ainsi dire* was brought out in an elegant edition by Éditions Finitude in 2004 and is the 'fourth' volume of the series.

Perros' short prose—whether aphoristic or somewhat more expansive—exhibits the author's recurrent themes: love, friendship, solitude, writing and death. And last but not least, God, scrutinized from an atheistic standpoint that nonetheless remains open to a dialogue that cannot exist by definition. God represents an absence that the poet takes into account only as a way of moving beyond this taking-into-account, beyond the temptation to entertain doubts; he seeks ways to live fully *without*. His many provocative maxims on the topic range from 'The epitome of pessimism: believing in God' to 'I'm sure that God exists. As for believing in Him, that's another matter.' Yet God is mentioned by Perros often enough to make one aphorism especially intriguing: 'If you don't believe in God, then you mustn't make use of Him in order to say you don't believe in Him.' Perros concentrated on the world at hand, especially on the men and women around him, but he seems never to have ceased facing up to and speaking about the ultimate Absence, rather as if this poet so sensitive to the spoken word were also challenged by Wittgenstein's injunction: 'Whereof one cannot speak, thereof one must be silent.'

As has already been suggested, Perros' focus on ordinariness, on the banalities of everyday life, is equally typical. What he termed 'the fact of our being daily' is an essential attribute of his literary vision. As to genre, the number and quality of his maxims illustrate his importance in the long French tradition of the aphorism, a lineage including Blaise Pascal, La Rochefoucauld, Chamfort, Joseph Joubert, Emil Cioran and Pierre-Albert Jourdan (who evokes in his own *Fragments* 'the genuine voice, the stylish voice of Perros the vagabond'). With typical modesty, Perros called himself a *journalier des pensées*, a day labourer who tills thoughts. Other short prose pieces indicate his excellence in related, sometimes hybrid, prose forms such as the diary-like entry, the vignette and the succinct critical perception. He is especially perspicacious on Mallarmé, a poet of whom one might not have initially thought in regard to him. Rimbaud's poetry and life are cited often. And he knew his Heidegger, perhaps another surprise for readers; yet Perros was interested in various philosophical fields, ranging from ontology and theology to social morals (and mores) and what used to be called philosophical anthropology. He was also a shrewd reader of Valéry, with whose *oeuvre* he carried on a lifelong dialogue and whose seminars at the Collège de France he had attended, as related in *An Ordinary Life*:

> There were very few of us
> Twenty-odd beautiful old biddies
> Three or four students and myself
> I sometimes read in literary reviews
> That those whom I never once noticed
> At his lectures and I didn't miss one
> During those war years are bragging
> About their having been there
> Where were they hiding?

This selection ends with Perros' famous *L'Ardoise magique* ('The Magic Slate'), a journal kept just before and after his cancer-stricken larynx was surgically removed. (The first edition was issued in 1978 by a small press, Givre, in Rimbaud's hometown of Charleville-Mézières, before being subsequently included in *Papiers collés 3*.) After his operation, Perros could communicate only with a piece of chalk and a small slate board. This journal is frequently cited because of Perros' at once poignant and detached style and because of his courageous lucidity about his plight as a speechless man awaiting death. Indeed, it is impossible not to think of the word 'courageous', but a further distinction must be made; and it suggests why the tone of 'The Magic Slate' is so particular. Perros declares now and then in his letters dating from the last two years of his life and specifically in 'The Magic Slate' itself: 'I don't need courage—a luxury. No, it's something else. Harsher.

More absolute. That you never need. Yet that's there.
The poor man's hidden savings. To be opened only
in an emergency.' Recalling the man's 'direst season'
in his tribute, Réda describes the small house that
the Douarnenez municipality had rented, beginning
in 1975, to Perros so that he could write in isolation.
It is located on Les Plomarc'h, the coastal heights
where the signpost now stands. Réda reports:

> I believed I'd go back up there one day, stand
>   before the bay,
> And knock on your door. One says 'one day,'
>   'soon'—
> Soon you spoke no more except with a piece
>   of chalk,
> Your verve galloping across a black surface.
> I prefer not to evoke that period
> When you showed us what a man could do
> By firmly remaining himself.

Reading *The Magic Slate* after many of the other
writings is particularly moving in that the French
word *parole*, which is rarely easy to translate—its
equivalents range from 'word(s)' and 'speech' to
'lyrics'—was a key term for Perros from the onset. In
both his poetry and his prose, his poetics engage with
'la parole' and 'voice' in all the senses of the terms.

Paper Collage has long enjoyed a cult status
among French readers and, especially, fellow writers.

Yet Perros has been completely overlooked in English (and other foreign languages), a situation that I deplored in an essay that was published in the *Antioch Review* (Summer 2000) and later reprinted as 'The "Tender Gesture" (Georges Perros)' in the first volume of *Paths to Contemporary French Literature* (2004). Critical studies of *Paper Collage* and other aspects of Perros's *oeuvre* include Jean Roudaut's *Georges Perros* (1991), Jean-Marie Gibbal's *Georges Perros, la spirale du secret* (1991), Jean-Charles Stasi's *Courant d'ouest* (1995), Gilles Plazy's *L'incognito de Douarnenez* (1999), Thierry Gillyboeuf's biography *Georges Perros* (2003), Yvon Béguivin's *Georges Perros et la Bretagne* (2004), Jean Lavoué's *Perros, Bretagne fraternelle* (2004), Marc Le Gros's *Sur Georges Perros* (2006), Daniel Kay's *Tombeau de Georges Perros* and the academic-essay collection *Lire Perros* (1995).

The secondary literature about Perros has never stopped growing. An important special issue of the *Nouvelle Revue Française* was devoted to Perros in September 1978, followed by special issues of the literary reviews *Bretagnes* (November 1978), *Encres* (1980) and *Ubacs* (February 1984), as well as the literary supplement of *Le Monde* (7 November 1980). Additional tributes comprise the Quimper exhibit catalogue *Hommage à Georges Perros* (1988) and the special issues of the reviews *Europe* (March 2011) and *Le Matricule des Anges* (July–August 2011).

Perros' books remain in print. *Une vie ordinaire* and the three-volume *Papiers collés* are available in popular Gallimard paperback editions. In the 1990s, his lively correspondence began appearing in separate tomes, gathering his letters to Gérard Philippe, the philosopher Jean Grenier, Jean Roudaut, Michel Butor, the poet Bernard Noël, Brice Parrain, Jean Paulhan, the poet-surgeon Lorand Gaspar and others. Self-effacing during his lifetime, Perros has clearly emerged as one of the lasting postwar French writers.

Translating his short prose is no easy chore. An analogy that would perhaps have pleased the amateur pianist is the difference between sight-reading and interpreting. The sight-reading initially seems not so difficult. But this is an illusion. Perros is working with the finest points of *la langue parlée*, not only at the semantic level but also at those of sound and social context. He offers insights into this phenomenon in several aphorisms and, most movingly, in the final passage of 'The Magic Slate':

> I'll have spent a great part of my life (the greatest part) attempting to draw out the unique tone of [men's] voices, rummaging through their private syntax, which lies at the farthest remove possible from the one making relationships possible in a time quickly recovered by politics, bookishness, trivial anecdotes. An amorous syntax needing

a wide field staked out for it so it can unfold (and be reassured). The musical score doesn't exist—you improvise as you play. A hesitant syntax. This is how two men engaged in a conversation come closer together, get lost, try each other out, one word opening the way to the next, in the unending twilight of the forest of raw language. (Cf. the echo of Weber's 'Wolf's Glen.') I'll have adored this peaceful hunt (my friends won't say the contrary) until I'm full, until the closing of the doors, the turning off of the lights.

I have tried to keep in mind such guidelines (and the writer provides others), hoping to capture in English some of the authenticity of this unique French voice. In the translations, it seemed necessary to establish a colloquial framework for diction which, at the same time, would allow abstractions, logical precision (in the aphorisms) and just a little poetic leeway in his somewhat longer prose texts. In the latter, there are a few instances of grammatical ambiguity that can be pinned down only by reading the prose aloud. Often, a text is 'of one piece' in this sense. This English *Paper Collage* offers many of Perros' maxims, a sampling of his most characteristic autobiographical writings and some of his succinct critical remarks. I have not included the book reviews, portraits, personal essays and travel pieces that also fill out the French volumes.

Nor have I rendered the long prefaces to the first two volumes of *Paper Collage*. The preface to the first volume comprises several sharp and humorous remarks about 'notes', the aphorism and the history of the genre. Readers of French should certainly look up these longer pieces. In the 'Notes' section, I have focused on allusions or references that might not be readily comprehensible to non-French readers. But I have not explained all of Perros' puns—not by a long shot! I have, however, endeavoured to find equivalents for them in English. In one case, where Perros writes about French grammar, I have him speak, in English, about English grammar. In another case, his pun about 'France', taken as a word, is transformed into a pun about the 'United States of America'.

This translation was greatly facilitated by a grant received from the National Endowment for the Arts in 2011. Let me reiterate my gratitude for this award. Frédéric Poulot, the poet's son, offered his encouragement from the onset of this project to these printed pages. Gillyboeuf generously answered questions and also chimed in with his encouragement. His critical biography was an excellent source of information, some of which I have used in the 'Notes'. Let me also thank Anne-Solange Noble of Éditions Gallimard and Thierry Boizet of the Éditions Finitude. Most importantly, progress on these versions would have been impossible without my wife, Françoise Daviet-Taylor, whom I consulted time and again during my attempts to advance from the 'sight-reading' to the interpretative stage.

John Taylor
Saint Barthélemy d'Anjou
2 February 2014

PAPER COLLAGE 1

I awake. Painlessly. I get up. All's well. I'm in good health. Yet this is normal. A fever would annoy me. However, it's impossible to retrace my steps and load the weight of the absent annoyance on the happiness scales. It's impossible to be happy about being happy.

✛

Creative work is never hopeless in that its impetus is positive.

✛

How can a work of art be human? Music be sad or merry? Everything that imitates life seems more human than what uses it. There's the future situation and the eternal situation.

✛

While other people sort us out, shove us as best as they can into their grinding mills, while the photo album gets a paunch, we age, inexorably progress towards whatever end awaits us and is impossible to foresee. Neither death nor solitude is a frightful phenomenon. I've often been amazed at the sight of human beings accepting death so calmly. As if a certain curve had exhausted its electrical and tangential powers. Atheists die even more tranquilly than believers.

✛

Love is when the body gathers momentum at the same time as the intellect, as knowledge, and just wins out though it's been fuelled by the latter, with the result that knowledge doesn't know whether it's lost the race or been enticed.

✛

The art of photography provides a fine symbol. You 'take' the landscape, the phenomenon or the face. You develop. Yet what needed light and exposure will be rendered only after its surrender, in darkness.

✛

Being alive means recording. What's called inspiration only consists of special moments in which human wax finds an appropriate needle.

✛

The greatest finesse lies in the least finesse. It's useless to make up a self since the epitome of a personal make-up, for others, is indeed naturalness. So few people are simple—in other words, lacking all emotional or intellectual provocation—that remaining as we are makes us unique.

✛

Everything worth living for is invisible and, para-
doxically, can be qualified only by an ideal third per-
son. Love and humour are phenomena that vanish
whenever they're detected. Their power is such that
we're allowed to speak about them as if we knew
what they were all about; as if language, at that level,
were as worthy as having experienced this sensation
coming down from on high. We say 'I love you' and
we've said everything. Yet we can legitimately say
this only insofar as we're not in love, that is, when
we're still conversant with or aware of possible words.
Only death seems to destroy all ambiguity. Saying
'I'm dead' is absolutely impossible. But saying 'I love'
is permissible. (Recommended.) Most admirable of
all is that when we love, when we're dispossessed, we
can let ourselves venture far enough to admit to it
without changing or disturbing anything whatsoever.
This is also why saying 'I don't love' in the same state
is like singing. When this state, which is musical par
excellence, depends on no outside enticement such
as women or alcohol, we're in the realm of poetry.

✢

Nothing is more natural than wanting to be loved
for oneself. And nothing sillier, since oneself doesn't
exist. Love is always approximate.

✢

Poem. A man is dying. DYING. He's transported to the clinic. He's saved. The operation is the poem.

✣

The best definition of man is found in La Fontaine, who was probably not claiming to formulate one: 'If a lute were playing all by itself, it would make me flee, though I have an extreme love for music.'*

✣

The earth is beautiful. The face of a human being sometimes comes close to our idea of a god made in our image. And despite all this happiness in our midst, beckoning us, someone, one day, dared to speak of the courage it takes to live. Someone, one day, killed himself. The brightest minds replied 'no' to the ultimate questionnaire. Perhaps not a single man, from the very beginning of mankind, has been willing to live again. Death is frightening, and almost all men leave without screams, without tears, without dread. Nothing resists the boredom, the fatigue, the wearing down of our sensibilities, not even all the charms dispensed by the flow of days and the various games we're given to play in this world. Just the time to fit out our interior in a rush, and the bell tolls. It's time to leave. To leave everything behind, lose every-thing, the woman whom we loved, the Nature that moved us so deeply. How can one fail to understand the thousands of 'what's the use?' that burst out and fade away in the indifference of space? At what degree of warmth, of suffering, of heartbreak does the 'what's the use?' cancel itself out, leaving a human being with no resources other than those of living beneath his own ruins and of no longer finding force except in his breathing, his very presence?

❖

Obsession with death sweeps life away as would a tidal wave. The torticollis of expectation then torments the human being who's left behind.

❖

In love, everything constantly cancels itself out. Everything needs to be begun again, in every instant. Two lovers dwell outside of time. Timetables are suspended. Death will never track down these hours that were brought to its attention. It will completely clean things out, but it will hunt in vain for its twin— the time of love.

❖

Nothing is more entertaining than the fate awaiting human beings who are determined to hide, to flee from others. Neither Valéry nor Rimbaud nor

Lawrence would have managed to become so universally well known so quickly had they desired such fame. Imitate them, you young people in quest of great glory. And if no one seeks you out, don't weep because you've succeeded where geniuses have failed. I'll not say another word.

✣

In order to live, we have to bend over and study—as well as rely on—a part of what perpetually passes through us and characterizes us. Why this instead of that? Why not be stupid, and continue to be so, since we're indeed stupid at times? We side with, that is, we endure what seems to suit our personal nature, which is the unknown par excellence yet which ends up hollowing out a rut in all this chaos. Therefore, I'll end up calling myself G. P. as a front. Living is therefore useless in that it's about pondering what has been found.

✣

There are individuals who inevitably implicate God, without pronouncing His name all that often, and whose existence is terribly angelic and seemingly chosen. I'm thinking of poets, especially Keats, Rilke, Rimbaud and Baudelaire. What they do 'here' can't be a criterion. They are themselves unaware of what drives them, what makes them suffer and live so *badly*. Such people make temperate Christians despair, for they appear to play leading roles in our tragedy without bothering whatsoever about 'scheming'. One expects these pure specimens to be winners, yet what an odd privilege this is—they're not believers but, rather, the believed.

❖

A maximum of simplicity goes with a maximum of difficulty as far as oneself is concerned. Being simple is not simple; it's attempting the impossible. I've never met simple individuals. And among the least gifted in this respect are those who say they're simple.

❖

At the dinner table. No one wants to eat the clams. My mother declares she'll never buy them again. I then feel invaded by an immense tenderness for clams, especially these. As I remember our buying them, coming home and preparing them, this 'nevermore' chills me with horror.* 'Serve me a few, after all,' I say to my mother.

❖

There are 'physical' impossibilities so insurmountable that the mind easily nullifies them without changing anything of their nature.

❖

In every great act of comprehension there's a part of gracious incomprehension that short-circuits intelligence.

✛

Seeing God wouldn't get us any further. Man is precisely the thing that gets no further because of this than because of that.

✛

What we are is what we think unwittingly and what guides us at the moment when we thought we were lost. Bird thoughts.

✛

If we're just a bit absent-minded, daytime goes by without a hitch. And we find ourselves in a horizontal position without having had the time to say 'whew'. It'd suffice to watch ourselves thus passing from day to night, tipping over ever faster, in order to understand a little more clearly what makes the human condition incomprehensible.

✛

Living all the time with another person, from morning to night, and after eight days we hate her. But living with oneself! So we go away on a trip, deigning to take a suitcase that would remind us of . . . And we arrive in a hotel room where the first thing noticed is a mirror. (No need to break it.)

✢

Writing is the richest, the most 'engaging' kind of action, the kind that musters the most elements to follow its movement. In contrast, pure and simple action is a mere trifle. Had Napoleon been able to become Chateaubriand,* he wouldn't have chosen the stopgap of civic and military heroism. Sleeping regretfully in every so-called man of action is the great poet he failed to be.

✢

Although literature makes waste, at least it has a chance of making a man stand straighter. It's important to understand this. Nearly all trades produce waste. Literature is one of the few occupations demanding rare willpower of a man, a way of running his existence that slows down the progress of a mediocrity that is natural to all of us.

✢

There's a phenomenon that actors know well and that consists of no longer 'thinking' the words of a play. In making the audience believe *they are there* whereas the words they pronounce are distinctly for-eign to their mental life which has been restored to its autonomy and has become vacant, as it were. If it were possible, they could almost think of something else (photo superimposed on photo) while they were spieling off their moving speeches, or stare at a fly in the theatre at the most pathetic moment of their monologues. I'd even say this condition is necessary *for being there* to the maximum. If a man is one with his act, he must necessarily die with it. It's easy to see that this is not the case.

⁜

What strikes me about a trial is the flood of words around silence. 'Did this woman kill her husband?' For days on end the truth will be sought, whereas the woman knows the answer and lets herself be encircled, attacked, defended. Every work of art is similarly conceived around silence, a knowing silence, but keeps the secret in order to allow the lie which apprehends it, which weaves it starting from the backside, which is supported by the lie, to take away all the bindings. 'Thus when I sucked the clarity of grapes . . .'*

⁜

Indifference withstands almost anything. And love really has a hard time extricating itself from it. Become indifferent in order to see if love withstands. Of course it withstands, to say the least. It occupies the whole field. It's love that is indifferent.

✣

The impossibility of loving without desiring to be loved in return withdraws all grace from this sentiment.

✣

Flood the present. We're air fish.

✣

Unlike Beethoven, Bach can't be listened to in groups of movements. He demands constant, rigorous attention. If we let him go, he lets us go. No 'poetic' passages. (The beauty is monotonous, tends to follow the flow of time.) Every note is at work, progressing by means of the strictest economy, so that they'll be counted up in the final sum. A cruel music. A music that says yes.

✣

Only death can impregnate a man. The face of a man who has slept with death and become 'pregnant' changes. Becomes jaundiced. Has shadows under the eyes. He's not going to last much longer. There are also miscarriages.

✜

Wishing to learn more than is allowed about a writer, about a singular individual, can be explained by a liking for murder. Donning your mask of psychology and *the love of truth*, you go down into the cellar, climb up into the attic. It can happen that you end up finding not a mote stashed anywhere. But read the writer's *oeuvre* more closely. You'll always end up finding the mote. The mote is literature. The beam is you, reading.*

✜

For a long time now, I've forgotten how to confide something important to another person. I thus speak in order to avoid silence. I relate anecdotes which are always listened to. The other fellow replies with his own stories, though he's perhaps silently thinking the same thing; and then we shake hands, both of us often burdened with words we'd like to shout. Yet what would be the use of bursting out with them? They're precisely the words that would be met with neither grace nor response. The weariness of explaining oneself, of talking about and finding faults with oneself and of taking advantage of friendship in order to make a show of one's suffering. But friendship lies in this phenomenon of self-modesty, in preventing oneself from saying everything to the one person in the world who would perhaps understand. Understand what?

✣

I'm obsessed with closed, autonomous spaces. I've never been able to write outdoors. And in my room—shutters closed, behind a folding screen, the light focused only on the piece of paper. A horror of mixtures. The mind can't bear life, its mighty enemy. Its remorse. And its principle. The mind always wants to say: 'I could easily get along without life.' Unfortunately, life is there, like a son who's been legally declared an adult and is staring at his parents.

✣

I think I've done everything—unwittingly—to avoid myself. To avoid my lucidity. I've tried everything to track down, then to flee from the sights of that terrible, imbecilic, pitiful human being, that Javert in pursuit of a wretched man.* But nothing enables me to go elsewhere, for this would mean following myself and awakening him; nor to kill this God or this Devil whom I periodically meet up with and who asks me for no explanation. Worst of all is his silence. Never blaming me. Never praising me. He takes everything in stride, both noble thoughts and evil ones. Lets me be free. And yet his very presence is a threat. The threat of his absence.

✣

I like it when I've drunk a little. I espouse the earth more easily. I spin a little. As for the earth, I seem sober. This state of half-drunkenness delights me. Just the right amount of coma. The one that I vainly sought with human beings, that I no longer hope to find except with myself, a day of rare special music, an accompanying music that will adopt me as the theme.

✣

I'm living like a tourist. I'm just passing through here. Unable to put in a token appearance. I stand facing other human beings as if they formed a land-scape. I delight in this, at a distance. Scarcely nothing but love asks for more. Alas, love is not at stake here. For months I've lost the sense of a lover's touch. For years, that of possessing a body. And I'm ageing, have no one to whom to give the long caress burning my blood. I have no Greek or Latin in which to express tersely all the underlying bitterness of this situation. And all my unwillingness that it be so.

✣

A reckless liking for failure. For death. A certain kind of death. That disposes me towards a reckless liking for life. Provided that life asks nothing of me. If I gamble, I'm afraid to win.

❖

When 'all is well', everything I imagine appears clearly, distinctly, to me. Not hazily, not caked with soot (motorcycle). Precisely, immediately. But I never know why I'm so perceptive. No diet to follow. If I begin living in the same way the next day—nothing. Such is the man, such is his work.

❖

The first man who thought of committing suicide humiliated life for all eternity. Life is like someone who remains greatly offended.

❖

Knowing what a human being is like means ceasing to complain about being one.

❖

Memory is like the mantel of a fireplace. Covered with curios that one must be careful not to break but that one can no longer see.

❖

What interests me is what escapes me. And what escapes me sizes up what I am.

✤

One has a sense of humour insofar as the other person notices nothing.

✤

Worriers who rent a seaside villa in order to pass on their worries to others.

✤

The epitome of pessimism—believing in God.

✤

We always invoke Heaven as our witness that we believe in nothing.

✤

We're our ideal contradictors. Our best enemies.

✤

Debussy wrote all his music while sitting in an aquarium.*

✤

I'm sure that God exists. As for believing in Him, that's another matter.

✣

Because life is incomparable, it's impossible to commit suicide.

✣

Discipline is loving what one loves.

✣

Man is the only ... thing of this world that raises its eyes to the sky as if it were asking a question.

✣

How to make the other person stupid without his noticing? Love him.

✣

All those whom we know though do not love are already dead.

All of us are already dead for many.

✣

It's as impossible to be good with others as nasty with oneself.

✣

Life will remain an uncertain thing as long as man exists.

✛

It takes the stupid a long time to understand; the intelligent, not to understand.

✛

Man, a sum of subtractions.

✛

You can get silence to shut up only by speaking less loudly than it does.

✛

There's no tight fit between man and the world, as between the door and its wardrobe.

✛

The body rests like a restless question.

✛

Life is a blind woman holding man on a leash.

✛

He made of her what she wanted.

✛

Sitting next to me in the cafe was a gentleman laughing while reading the *Financial Times*.

✣

Modern education class. Say three times: God is dead. Life is absurd. A revolution is necessary, etc. Very good. Now you can go and play marbles.

✣

Writing implies giving up the world while imploring the world not to give us up.

✣

It's as incredible to be alone as not. Our bodies fill the hole our minds keep deepening. (One fine day, the body is overtaken—goodnight all!)

✣

It's as stupid to kill yourself as to love. A misunderstanding always induces the act. Suicide nullifies a part of ourselves by removing the whole. Love exalts this same part. Love is the exact opposite of suicide. Either kill someone in ourselves or love that someone in someone else.

✣

Friendship begins with medicine. We palpate each other: 'Where does it hurt, etc.' Then it's time for

•

surgery. Finally we arrive at the heart of the subject, or the object, and off you go—we amputate! The next gentleman, please.

✢

Platonic love. I've experienced it with my friends. A friend who says 'I'm fond of you' moves me as much, and as completely, as a woman who makes me understand that this is her feeling for me. But with men I retain the emotion. I swallow it. A woman necessarily implies some kind of future. It's she who represents the hope of the emotion.

✢

Love is not the opposite of hate. It's its sublimation.

✢

Love makes one do things that annul love.

✢

Wittiness strictly means being unaware of what you're going to say in five minutes.

✢

Advice. If you can give some, it'd be better to refrain from doing so. The matter is unimportant.

✢

Curiosity, the bee of ignorance.

✤

Shot by a firing squad. Don't play blind man's buff with men.

✤

Loving means giving someone the right, if not the duty, to make us suffer.

✤

We applaud. Then we applaud ourselves for applauding. The applause keeps going on. Thunderous applause is more difficult to interrupt than thunderous insulting.

✤

The possibility of committing suicide prohibits complaining and justifies boredom.

✤

The worst thing that can happen to God is that man no longer calls His existence into question. This is also the worst thing that can happen to man.

✤

Idleness, the mother of all vices and the daughter of all virtues.

✜

Music. You hold your head in your hands in order not to think.

✜

Silence is the actor's reward.

✜

Genuine time is nocturnal. I wind my watch in the evening.

✜

As soon as a human being becomes aware, he's worked over by death, as wood is by a worm.

✜

I've unwittingly preserved this naivety: when I open a book, I like it to be a book. I expect literature. Otherwise, life suffices—that is, me and other people. If the purpose of reading is to find yourself back in life, then telephoning your neighbour and spending an evening talking nonsense is just as worthwhile. We all have an idea of what literature is or should be. Some people read to escape. (From what prisons?) Others to learn.

(To what ends?) Still others read because it's more worthwhile to spend time with a man's written language than with the spoken language. Hence: I don't detest my concierge, but I'm fond of Mallarmé. Both Mallarmé and my concierge strike me as plying their trades, with the usual drawbacks.

✣

'If God does not exist, everything is permitted.'* I think what is frightful is that everything is permitted even if He does exist.

✣

We're willing to bring happiness to others. But we're not very happy—despite what one says—when the same others get involved in our happiness.

✣

God is not the only thing, if you will, preceding any thought. Some men seem to begin to live only when their conscience gets set into motion. Such are philosophers. Others think, are able to think, only by beginning with their childhood. Their thinking has the scent of, seems held back or delayed by, childhood impressions.

✣

How to write interesting things to someone who won't fail to find them interesting?

✣

It's disappointing to be believed. Even when you tell the truth. Especially when you tell the truth.

✣

The accompaniment is the enemy of the theme. The latter will swallow up the former.

✣

Only a woman can give me the will to work again. And only work can get me to give up women.

✣

I sense only absences.

✣

Not only do I not need to see the human beings I love in order to love them, I need to not see them. But do they continue to love me? So, we see each other again.

✣

Having nothing to hide except that you've nothing to hide.

✣

Writing brings no cure—it exaggerates the illness. Like squeezing a pimple that's about to burst.

✥

If you don't believe in God, then you mustn't make use of Him in order to say you don't believe in Him.

✥

Hope is not prompting another person to say what you'd like to hear him saying. Hopelessness is also this.

✥

History.

Every day the trains go by at the same hour. And yet, every day the level-crossing keeper is surprised.

✥

Don Juan is the man* a woman thinks of when she's in the arms of a man. Even if this man is Don Juan.

✥

My dream, which can easily be carried out, would be to write whatever comes to mind on little cards, like visiting cards, all the while forbidding myself to use more than one of them for every such time I think of something. I'd toss the cards into a box and, every fifty years, sort through them. I'd assign each a number.

❖

It's difficult to kiss a woman without rubbing away the red she has on her lips.

❖

Making mistakes in English is not important, of course.* But will you love a woman you're getting ready to love if, as you're entering a restaurant, you hear her say: 'This one is inferior than the other'? Perhaps you'll correct her: 'No, darling, "inferior to".' 'Oh, you and all your fine distinctions!' The evening will be difficult to get through.

❖

I don't think that love is necessary—rather, it's the opposite—for making a world in which love is possible.

❖

I'm surely an irritating fellow. A few reasons for this:

I don't like what I write. I write.

Only solitude suits me, like a garment that excludes neither scarf nor coat.

I feel quite normal, understand nothing about my difficulties.

Love needs to be reinvented.* I agree.

Every day, I've the distinct sensation—the most distinct of all my sensations—that I've had it. Impossible to right the tiller. Which rights itself. This is a little annoying.

‡

It's probably true that the world is hateful, since so many influential personalities have declared it to be so. Among other thinkers, moralists have never said anything else, as if stating this allowed them to live a day longer. Solitude has always been negative. Living in society leads to suicide. Which by no means prevents us from having friends and from bearing the 'I love you' of the opposite sex. So? Are we able to love for a long time? Be loved for a long time? No. So? We play. But at what? No game has two winners. A useless nil draw? Yes, nil and useless. So how can we *make* love?

‡

Paying attention. It's the opposite of an event. Subsequently, the event becomes the counterpoint. The event, a crime. Saturation of the anecdote.

‡

The drama of life is that it can happen that nothing happens.

✣

To be, not all the ideas of a man—let him keep them—but, rather, all the men of an idea.

✣

A tender person who has militarized his tenderness. One quickly becomes a field marshal while playing this game. And one wins, for all eternity, the impression of being 'hard to get along with'.

✣

The most obvious thing is forgetting. Every day we need to go back down the same road leading to our limits.

✣

Sometimes in the evening, I feel like giving our dear Lord a ring on the telephone. I'm serious.

✣

Writers whom we get to know after reading their *oeuvre*. The other writers. No connection between them. We never manage to recover. All the more so in that they're our elders. Between young writers, the *oeuvre* doesn't exist.

✣

What's annoying about literary criticism is that it judges something that cannot change.

✣

Some human beings 'carry more weight' than others. Good, even excellent, writers exist. So much the better for them. Others couldn't be excellent writers if they tried, yet they're likely to shake up your mental monolith by means of twenty difficult pages. Poetically. See Heidegger.*

✣

You could perhaps meet a woman who looks like Mona Lisa, but Mona Lisa obviously doesn't look like any other woman.

✣

Writing letters is dangerous. You write affectionate (or even worse) messages to individuals whose presence you wouldn't be able to bear. No hypocrisy is involved. You have affection for them, at a remove. Yet if they follow up on your epistolary effusions and announce their arrival, you grow pale. This is otherwise only one of a thousand subtleties, as big as roof beams, which turn our relationships with others into a series of fevers and chills. You need a strong pair of lungs.

✥

Writing means venturing beyond one's capabilities. Whence lying and ethics. No man can write without laying bare his possibilities, his limitations. The man feels so slight that he finds respite only by exaggerating this slightness. He thereby sometimes attains art which, albeit far from ridding him of his misery, emits a fragrance. Beauty exists, but it's not a form—it's a sensation.

✥

As soon as a man *feels* eternity, the moment falls off the hook.

✥

Write while it's hot.

✥

You can't force yourself to love, and love is precisely this.

✥

You can't bear others without bearing yourself, and trying to bear yourself by means of others is deadly.

✣

It's interesting to notice that the thought of dying is least painful when life is in full swing.

✣

If I lose my dignity with Y, I recover it with X who does not know Y.

✣

Any woman putting me into an erotic state makes me want to make love with another woman.

✣

Mozart. How the note is attacked. Above. Diction. Energy. Stendhal.

✣

Writing is the least pessimistic act of all.

✣

Man has no prestige, and this is what makes him wish for a god who would remember his great deeds which other human beings are incapable of retaining. You perform some mighty feat in the neighbourhood cafe. You enter the one next door. There they treat you as they know you. This is what explains solitude.

✛

I love, love not, can love only God. But human beings will know nothing of this. (Nor God.)

✛

What worries the cat is motionlessness.

✛

I get white thoughts into my head.

✛

It's as if the pleasure of being alive couldn't really develop—not in another world but indeed in this one—unless we were absent from it.

✛

Your thoughts while telephoning. While you're dialling up your little show.

✛

It would be good if a journal could be written in the same way that Picasso paints. A distorting journal that would show artistry without losing sight of the obvious martyrdom that results from our being our own ghostwriter, especially in matters of sensibility, which rules us, decrees us, drives us.

❖

I make no perceptible difference between friendship and love. Both have made me suffer. The physical difference is that friendship makes us suffer like a toothache that only half declares its existence and whose pain remains bearable. As for love, I no longer remember.

❖

Lying deifies the other person.

❖

Human beings clearly go to a lot of trouble to be unhappy. Yet are they?

❖

Living in the provinces. You can't imagine the extent to which receiving news *too late* nullifies the seriousness of events. To the extent that we realize how helpless we are in regard to their evilness. But man is a province incomparably further away than any exile.

❖

A cheerful diary is unimaginable. When a human being bends over himself, peers into his immediate past, he catches only the disastrous fish.

✢

Objectivity is saturated subjectivity. But being objective before stuffing yourself sick with subjective matter is like entering a church because it's raining.

✢

God exists. He's the lack of everything save 'of everything'—and safe from everything.

✢

Precise language removes man from a dream in which he's been, from the beginning, the broken-down mannequin.

✢

PAPER COLLAGE 2

To reach what we think, we have to go beyond our limits. The results are our very limits.

✣

Every day I tell myself that things are going to change. And every day I ask myself why things should change. Difficult mornings. Possible evenings.

✣

What's a truth that is not called into question every day? Writing often masks this urgent matter. Some novelists tackling a new book tell themselves: Two or three months of peace and quiet ahead of me, let's hope for even more.

✣

You always write only an inch away from stopping to speak.

✣

The worst thought: I can only do what I'm doing.

✣

I've come here to spend New Year's Day somewhat on the sidelines. T's gone to bed. I took my motor-cycle and I'm writing to you from a small bistro. At a stone's throw from the sea, as the other fellow says.

In the farmyard there are hens, slumbering dogs; mooing cows can be heard; not a soul outside, except for the souls of a few real cats. The weather is mild, almost like spring. I think I have a wife and kids yet something prevents me from fully believing so, from being certain, because life scarcely allows certainties, even of this kind. As always, I find myself between two train stations, no longer young but as if stricken with infantilism, having so greatly loved what I love and so greatly detested what I hate. Here, perhaps, is a semblance of coherency that would justify, however slightly, my odd presence. Sometimes I panic when sensing how much of a social outcast I am, and I hang on only to friendship. Since T., in any event, is excluded from the world of men (and women!), I can consider her to be only my daughter, and I'm afraid she'll be run over when crossing the street. (Ah, if she were listening to me!) I had the same sensation with my parents. This implies no need for authority, or paternity! Good God no! But rather a strange kind of tenderness for the human beings I love, and a fear they'll be handed over to the horror of being alive; a horror I've brushed up against in daydreams or, with my eyes shut, in dreams, as I approached regions, chasms, caves where language is moth-eaten, gobbled down, gnawed at, by the rats of death.

More customers have entered the bistro. Two fish-ermen alongside me now. In the next room some kids are watching television. The cows continue to chew. The hens couldn't give a damn. What's stupider than a hen? They're made to be eaten. Happy New Year all the same.

✣

Those moments when all the books and human beings in the world become insufficient. When, in a fully stocked library, you wouldn't find a single lifeline-book, even as a shipwrecked sailor finds no rescuing hand to grasp. Those moments indeed give us an idea of death. Strangely, at the same time, they unveil life in its extreme nudity, and the passion we have for it. There's nothing worse. But nothing better. You know you'll have to *return* to them, for such moments come and go without warning. Leaving us with a kind of memory, like the taste, the aroma, on the palate, of a very rare wine.

✣

There's no pleasant place to go to since our body prevents us from going out.

✣

I can act well enough in the wings. I was doomed to write, a solitary act. As soon as someone looks at me, I'm done for.

✢

Renard, indeed, because of his sharp vision, his quick ferociousness—and let me take a foxy bite out of your leg of language.* The Romans had their Julius. We have our Jules. I hadn't grasped this until a performance of *Plaisir de rompre*. In the very middle of the play, crashing noises in the theatre. It was a bat hurling itself against the walls, wounding itself. Flying, yet unable to find the window. I understood my Jules Renard.

✢

I have an excellent memory. I retain almost nothing.

✢

Suicide doesn't mean wanting to die but, rather, wanting to disappear.

✢

When I'm far from my friends, I always believe they're doing extraordinary things (which sometimes happens). But when we're together, it's as if my very presence prevented them from doing so.

✢

I sometimes happen to think things that *normally* I shouldn't be thinking. They surpass me. What should I do with these thoughts? A few months, even a few years later, I realize that they concerned me, that they were my limits in a state of liberty. That these *thoughts*, or *ideas*, dwelt in other human beings, paid their rent for them, but that by *brushing up* against me, by alighting like birds on my solidest branch, they let me know that, despite my mental weakness, I depended on them. And that at the same time, they depended on me, for as long as a halt takes between two long journeys.

✢

At this stage, I'd say that what has seemed the most difficult thing to do is to love what we love, to keep intact the why of a choice, for this why tends to get lost in the thousand-and-one caverns of our fallacious enticements. It's thus necessary to *work* at preserving it, and the word 'work' scarcely has any other meaning for me—that one. Working at not willingly smothering what bothers us. And love bothers us.

✢

It can happen that I've nothing to say, but never that I've nothing to write. For writing involves gestures and participates in a possibility which is only rarely euphoric yet which, like walking, is indispensable to one who has become sensitive to it only once. It's a sport, a kind of exercise, in Valéry's sense of the term.* When I'm not writing, I get fat, like an athlete who thickens out as soon as he gives up his daily training. And at the same time, the ambiguous pleasures of competition are removed. For we're built in such a way that what we can accomplish on our own ends up becoming an utter failure. Imagine a gentleman who could high jump more than seven and a half feet. Now imagine him alone in a deserted place, jumping for his own pleasure. It's unimaginable. We need to rub shoulders with others, if only to complain about them. As to their glorification, this must quickly become fastidious. But it's impossible to avoid it, and nothing dooms us more readily, for we are incapable of lasting tenderness and friendship. No human being seems likely to suffice for our mediocrity as well as for our virtues. And we need human beings other than our friends in order to define us in the very temporary absolute that characterizes our lives. You expect 'criticism' from a friend, but of a secondary kind. It's criticism from an unknown person that affects us. And the friend will vanish. The appetite we have for human beings who are able to tell us what our place is in their mental space resembles the desire making us move from one woman to another, because settled-in love doesn't last long. We need to be resuscitated, and whoever loves us is doomed in advance. We want to be loved, but not always by the same man or woman. This is what makes our lives difficult. How to get out of this mess?

✢

I've never done anything except out of pleasure. This states well enough that I haven't done much.

✢

How to go back into your body? Other people make us take shelter inside it, rather than simply going back into it.

✢

He collected the cigarette butts of celebrities.

✢

Sex is a thousand women. A woman is a thousandth of sex.

✢

I've lots of friends, but I wouldn't like to die, or even feel sick, in their company.

✢

I don't dare to begin because I wouldn't like to finish.

✤

Writing always means being the ghostwriter of someone you'll never meet.

✤

You speak of your children in the future tense.

✤

All the words are in the dictionary.* Or almost all. Hence, if I want to write like Rimbaud or Lautréamont, all I have to do is choose. What's writing if it's not reaching one's limits and, by this very act, freeing oneself from them? The more gifted one is at handling words, the greater the choice. Enter Hölderlin, Mallarmé, Artaud. All those accursed poets. But can you imagine Mallarmé *beginning* with the *Coup de dés*, Hölderlin with *Scardanelli*, Artaud with . . . nothing? No. You can't choose a vocabulary of malediction on the pretext that it's the only efficient one. Living is useful for that. Living is useful, if only to write that you spit at life. Life *permits* everything. Including suicide.

✤

A man has several languages. Even as a woman has several bodies. You can't guess the language of nighttime caresses by referring only to that of daytime encounters. What's 'heard', 'understood', as language is therefore deceitful, veiled, and lacks, for example, what we demand of reading, attention at that level implying another, solitary kind of attention. If human beings had no possibility of solitude, they'd be in hell. All we do is perceive the horror; yet we're granted the time it takes for this perception. Solitude is allowed. And we don't want it. We even go so far as to insult those who withdraw from the ever-rising tide—with no ebb—of evil, of the terror two human beings decree as soon as they bind themselves together, as soon as they think the pact is possible. Friendship is of a nostalgic nature. Love is rather the opposite—it will come. While waiting for that love, while scratching away at that nostalgia, we graze on the present like a cow in a pasture; we snap up the sky, like any bird on its branch.

✛

My life is a happy suicide.

✛

Impossible to be the friend of a priest, a communist, a doctor. Why?

✛

He sometimes replied: 'Excuse me, but I won't be able to come and see you next week. I'll be sick.'

❖

A poet has no memory. But is one.

❖

I like to drink. Any wine. Good beer. Strong alcohol. I hate all aperitifs, perhaps because of the word. I've never drunk 'to forget', out of despair or idleness. I like everything that's liquid. The sea. Fluidness. Anything that's in motion. Fresh. There's spontaneity in the surging forth of a source.* A spontaneity that's finely crafted, of course. I like the bar counter of a bistro; it provides a way of approaching human beings from a distance, of listening to them, of looking at them without running the risk of being taken for something other than the shape of a man in transit. It's a little like being in train stations. And I like the time that goes by between getting off one train and waiting for the next one. I inhale life fully into my mind, into my body, since I realize this is fleetingness and 'what's going to end' because of the journey, not because of saturation, as in kinds of laborious immobility. I'm a man of in-betweenness, always fidgeting, and if I write, it's in the margins. The text is elsewhere. I've accustomed myself to this impotency. It suits me well. In this regard, my coquetry could be evoked without shocking me. I'm essentially a man of the theatre wings. I hate acting on stage and I hate being in the audience. But I feel fine when I'm merely an inch away from both. I thus love the sea, but would I ever be a seaman? I like men who like what I like, though I'm unable to stand their too-insistent presence. With women, it's of course much more complicated. You have to act. To go back into matter, which I execrate, which for me is death—to make a show, to pretend, to force your body to thrust into the nothingness of the spasm. It took me time to get my ego to come along with me—this ego that's always where I'm not. It was hard to get everyone together, to send the appropriate telegrams. Now everything is more or less all right. I fathered children with a woman who puts up with me. I feel neither more nor less present. But amazed. (As well one might be.) Here, that big word 'love' loses all its execrable meaninglessness in order to cover—recover—a meaning that's the very one of life, of the movement that characterizes it. My child is water—indeed, why not sperm—submitted to a treatment by operation. With the woman acting as the text.

✤

What we can best demand of a book is that it demands to be read again. Until we've read it to death. We'll never have read it. There's something untranslatable in language. This is its very force. Like that of *Nature*. There's Nature in language. Nothing 'natural'. Just Nature. So why the devil do we sign our names to what we write?

✣

When my dog sees me completely naked, it doesn't recognize me.

✣

How to go back and meet the being that's behind us?

✣

Language is not made with language—as an omelette is with eggs—but we can, and this is what literature is all about, draw out from the universal language— the one spoken by our neighbour as well as by the most remote human being—that special language that catches fire at the slightest happenstance, provided the event is grasped ahead of time. I can accept the notion that everything comes from, and goes back to, language. But when the event *turns into* language, opts for or takes refuge in language, then, yes, let's say it enters 'poetryhood'; there are always a few weak, speechless reasons for this. Poetry is like a dog that would suddenly find itself invaded by speech and streak over to those who knew how to speak in order to have them translate what it hears with such confused astonishment. This dog—or any other speechless person!—exists in every human being. He lacks only the speech that we refuse to let him have. Or that we don't know how to translate.

✢

We find out a little about the lives of other people, our fellow creatures (as one strangely says), only when they're dead. At that point, you can't believe how much you learn about what they needed to account for—whereas no valid information reached us while they were among us. People who write autobiographies are always criticized for telling us the story of their own lives. But actually they've only got one fault. That of thinking we're going to believe them. For the fact of living has something unbelievable about it that goes from one human being to the next. In order to be 'ratified', the man who opens himself up so foolishly—if he ever imagines that his life is going to change because he recounted it to his neighbour—must die. There's only one radical way to change your life—die. Let yourself die unto yourself. Make yourself into that Other evoked by Rimbaud, whose 'I' probably declared itself when he'd specifically become that Other.* Yet Rimbaud, first and foremost, hardly ever stopped telling us his life's story. *A Season in Hell* is an extraordinary autobiography. Yet addressed to no one. Indeed, to no one. Unless to those who were like the protagonists concealed, blended or metamorphosed in the dazzling words. Verlaine doubtless didn't read *A Season in Hell* in quite the same way we do. Every piece of writing is addressed to a living person who may well be unable to recognize or meet up with himself in it. This matters little. There are no 'imaginary' creatures for the simple reason that we—you and me, all of us—are imaginary creatures. Children know this very well. One of my sons calls me Mr Sausage one day, Mrs Elephant the next. To the extent that, in the street, I no longer know how to 'state' my personal particulars. This is probably why we're obliged to have an identity card. It's useful. Not only for policemen but also for ourselves. So we can exist. Can have a head unlike the heads of others. Fingerprints. Hair colour. And aren't we also assigned numbers? Registered? How's that for differences! When human beings will all wear the same uniform, we won't be able to recognize ourselves any more. The differences will be at their maximum. Exactly as if we chose to stop wearing clothing. Difficult.

✣

At school, whenever the teacher didn't completely erase the blackboard, the overlooked chalky scribble made me sick for the rest of the day.

❖

Valéry claimed that the first line comes from the gods.* No, it doesn't. The first line comes from human beings. What illuminates and determines this region that is decreed poetic indeed appears and is triggered only by man. Gods take care of what follows in order to preserve the lyrical ambiguity of the lightning bolt. Moreover, Valéry let the cat out of the bag. His best poems are precisely those for which he let the gods finish what he'd begun well, and you can begin a poem anywhere. In short, man attacks, and the gods wish, or accept, to join in the battle or not. Man all by himself is less poor than God all by Himself. It's even been stated that God had needed man, though this is perhaps excessively exaggerated. Let's say that man and God wouldn't know how to do without each other, without mutual injury.

The great poet is the one who gets the greatest number of gods working. It's impossible to count the number of gods employed by Shakespeare or Browning. In the craftsman's sense of the term, a masterpiece is probably this. A joint effort resulting from a human decision which sets the tone.

❖

Without being very sharp, you can imagine all human beings want to be free, and not unhappy. This is false. They want their own freedom, not their neighbour's. They want their happiness, or unhappiness, not their neighbour's. When two freedoms meet, it's war.

✣

The need to write comes back as a chance. Or an illness. A chance to find the lost paradise once again. An illness, for the more one writes the less one finds the lost paradise. And it's quite difficult to preserve the energy that orders us to write, to not lose it once the writing is done.

✣

I'm sometimes asked, and it's nice of those who do so, why I don't write novels. Characters . . . Writing is like sleeping, but in the opposite direction. I enter writing completely armed. I launch myself into the composition. But the lack of adversaries brings me to a rather quick halt. Genius depends on the greater or lesser number of adversaries, of obstacles to hurdle. Mine are *elsewhere*, not in writing, but writing retains them. Shows them to me. And I need to see clearly, in darkness. As little as nothing. Whence the note.

✣

I can't live in opposition to what I write. I'm the absolute contemporary of my writings. Words settle in me, and threaten. This is probably why I'm called a moralist. Poetry is adequacy. A word set down crookedly, a new wrinkle.

✣

Is it by chance that what's essential in music comes from Central Europe, far from the sea? I don't think so. The sea engenders no echoes. And echoes constitute all of *classical* music—the forest, Salzburg. You can't imagine either Mozart or Beethoven without a forest. Especially Beethoven. His sonatas run through woods, with sudden clearings, shadowy spots, streams, flights, twilights.

✣

I understand life as a long conversation that should never end between human beings and things. A more or less acute, elaborate conversation, as in life which is a kind of aquarium. But speaking to and being with others implies sticking your nose out of the aquarium, even leaving it. In order to follow another person. Who gets you to enter his or her aquarium. This is what's called love. Two human beings in love with each other quickly become asphyxiated. This is normal. You have the impression they do so on purpose. That they love each other—and go out—only in order to rush into the sentimental aquarium where they suffocate in devious ways. Then there are other kinds of people, the lukewarm ones, who never leave their aquariums and couldn't care less about doing so. From which follows the solitude of poets, scholars and madmen. Death wouldn't know how to surprise them. It will have been their life.

✛

Man can get an idea—let's leave the word vague—of the earth which is his thing. He can easily play at solving outer riddles, boldly trying to fashion for himself alone a little planet with its thousand climates, colours, skies. For example, he can put into an eastern prince's mouth twelve metrical feet strongly influenced by dramatic cosmopolitanism: 'In the deserted East . . .'* Here, Racine treats himself to a free trip that would be quite difficult to take in a barouche, even more so in a boat because of pirates. I even wonder if the most superior, indeed economically most superior, means of seeing everything, of taking delight in everything, doesn't consist of renting a room built up against a wall, with neither sky nor horizon in view, and in living there without fussing about furnishings. Or about the surroundings. A human being's eye takes on its essential function, and is justified, only if it 'looks out on' another human being with whose own eye it gets married, into a swirl, a dance or a fight. Seen more than seer, a human being must turn many well-known pages before daring to say he's taken delight in a landscape. I've always avoided, like the plague, group excursions that have selected a handful of individuals for the summit of a mountain, or the shore of a lake, with tour guides on the promontory. The Ahs and Ohs of my companions create just as many laughable and irritating reasons to take French leave. But in all things, I need to putter around in the garden of my zoological acclimatization. Me and not me, for who composes and decomposes the inner kaleidoscope, who decides how it's arranged and smoothes things out? It behooves you to let others—call them whatever you wish: angels or demons—do what we'd be incapable of humanizing without running the risk of overly anecdotal jealousy or narrow-mindedness. Let's give full powers to our complementary difficulty, let it become autonomous in our no-man's-land. Let the difficulty mingle in our nervous fairs whenever it wants to. One morning, over the washbasin. One afternoon, at the movies. One evening, in a street. One night, in the arms of a woman. Naturally, the moments when we might head into these rays of intelligence that totalize us are unpredictable.

And feminine. Let's not go running after them. No pose, no smile, no faithfulness can get the better of them. Secretly linked to our most sensitive epidermis, they like nothing less than uprightness and willpower. Chasing after them, honestly, is useless. They scent a game and hopes of being rewarded. Better to ignore them. They're more ours than we are. Better to let them play truant than give them a mental education. Let them sprout, as if our soil bore roots and dizzily blossomed. Who knows?

✣

If you've ever once been in a euphoric situation, and usually the euphoria doesn't depend on other human beings, you don't really know how to retain this beneficial moment inside yourself, to renew its lease. So you write. You don't write to recover it. You write in order to prevent *everything else* from obstructing the possibility of such a moment taking place. This is why poets, who are devoted to this moment, never make progress. Why their first poem can be as good as their last one. Why there's no hierarchy in their itinerary, since the goal lies at the beginning, not the end. They write in order to preserve a vast impressive knowledge, not to acquire it. They're on the lookout in order to preserve this unstable equilibrium that life with adults—and they're themselves adults—

makes difficult. Inspiration, their inspiration, comes from this. From afar. Every time they touch the thread of it, they quiver, but it's not a discovery. It's a confirmation. Living and dying coming out even.

❖

Speech comes from a dream. But man is a dream. We contemplate one another as we'll never be able to contemplate Nature which has no equal. We look at one another as if we were idiots and morons who were merely astonished, alarmed or threatened, and sometimes delighted. Words come from man's permanent dream, which another man shows up to interrupt, and a dream rarely opts for an exchange, a conversation. When a dream deigns to get mixed up in one, we can relax. We're persuaded that whatever the other person's response, however humiliating or wounding, we'll never have to do anything else than go back to what we've actually never left—our dream. To take up once again that strange monologue, with its thousand and one voices, which we're used to calling solitude and which must be the absolute opposite. My speech doesn't touch the depths of my solitude—they converse with each other. It's when I have the misfortune to connect the organic obscurity of my solitude with human contact that an abscess forms. All alone, I don't wound myself at all. I wouldn't be able to do so. I'm incapable, and it's a luxury. Suicide lies at the end of this incapability.

✤

He said softly what he thought out loud.

✤

After all, I'm not much good for anything. I realize this more and more often. I'm almost a suicide case. I live on the seashore, but ask me to sail and I'm unable to do so. I keep making a woman pregnant who didn't ask for as much because she already had a few children, but if needed I would be damn unable to help her give birth. Despite this, I don't feel like a bastard, yet my lack of fundamental *human* knowledge sometimes makes me miserable, and the word is weak. What I *know* how to do doesn't take place on the daily marketplace, and this knowledge is so meagre, so shaky, that it's far from reassuring me about the validity of my presence. I've thus fled—an easy, simple thing to do—from the human beings who were capable of making me interesting. I was thought to be rather eccentric, but I knew what I didn't want. I remain face to face with what I want. I've ended up understanding that I wanted nothing. And that I was always given something. That made me exist. The obsession with freedom that has driven me, this perpetual movement of mine—it's been satisfied. I'm free. Human beings can say whatever they want, they can hurt me—it's nothing. They can't do anything but good to me now (I got 'em!). They're doomed to doing nothing but good to me. Actually, I wanted to say: Here I am, all alone. Without the slightest nostalgia or bitterness. Without *anything*. I'm no crazed lover of Nature, nor of this object, this passing woman. Death will have no difficulty invading me. I'll have done its work for it.

✣

Poetry is like a naked woman walking down the Champs-Elysées in broad daylight without being noticed. Without being seen. Except, briefly, by the blind.

✣

My *literary* fault, of course, is to let everyone speak, all those distraught human beings moving around inside me and going by my unique, pitiful name. Genius would probably consist in putting them on stage in a play or novel. In this way, I could avoid the contradictions, the too-numerous fevers and chills, the short circuits. In this way, I could avoid people taking me for a shilly-shallyer. And avoid taking myself for one! I write while being hounded by someone who's suddenly awakened and asked to be given the floor. I stop speaking and give the floor to this poor wretch who has landed inside a poor wretch who knows a little French.

✣

There's suicide. That's pretty good. But one should have thought of its opposite.

✣

Being free? Indeed, why not? Everyone can choose his desert.

✣

Friendship is like love. It has its moments of crisis and insanity, its absurdity, its redoubtable logic, its end. We've all written dozens of pages to friends who immediately replied with as many pages. That's what youth is all about. Talking about yourself in the future tense to a contemporary who is as old are you are.

✣

You have a rendezvous at 2 p.m. with a friend whom you haven't seen for ten years and who's close to your heart. You run into him by chance, at 1 p.m., at the house of some common friends. This botches it all up. Definitively. Why?

✣

What I call poetry is an opportunity to go to, or detour through, whereabouts in which I never could or should have gotten lost without poetry. Poetry leads me astray without warning. Once a decision has grabbed me, my own language runs the risk of losing its quasi-social position in order to venture into regions of which it knows nothing, particularly the *language*. Where it will have to *get by* on its own. There are people who manage this very well and very fast. But I'm no Rimbaud. (One would have noticed!) So I waited until my words lined up like Panurge's sheep, in a *real* way, and I followed them.*

✣

What makes Mallarmé a poet different from others, from all the others, is not his genius, which is inferior to that of many poets, but rather—and this is where it becomes difficult, almost impossible to express— his sensitivity to the nothingness, the non-being, the nihility of what creates and undoes the relationships that human beings maintain among themselves.* A society according to Mallarmé is hard to imagine, but we know all too well, every day, why it's inconceivable. Mallarmé has death under his skin, and it's no bluffer; he harbours inside himself a kind of deep regret that he lives in a dead space. Since he's not Nietzsche, he makes no thunderous declarations; he doesn't decree a funeral for God, but the essentials of everything he says is informed, and defined, by this demise, which leaves man grappling with the horror and the glory of being. For this reason, he'll always be ready to use pure language to compose his *Tombeaux*. The extent to which one doesn't count on God in order to write can't be stated better.

✢

The possibility of an absolutely withdrawn language, a language that would be dead yet resuscitated. Dead before it's dead, its poetic power topples over into what lies beyond its coming into being.

'There is a dead human being, a grave, the words of a dead child, who has become our honour, the source of our best sentiments.'

Mortuary language. Anatole's death comes at the right *grave* moment.* Horribly so.

Reality, for Mallarmé, lies beyond presence. It imposes absence on what it sees in favour of a resurrection by means of words which are reflected instead of being reflected upon. Nothing is more efficient, more endowed with *hardness* than Mallarmé's perpetually re-creative vision. Whence his propensity for tombs and tomblike tributes. Absolute celebration in the coffin of language.

✢

Work is the obstinate search for the *moment* when you don't have to work in order to be inspired.

❖

I live. I exist. I'm here. If I fall, I hurt myself. Others can make me suffer. I know I'm going to die. That I'm more pathetically than socially responsible for a wife and three children. I'm neither happy nor unhappy. These words hardly make sense to me any more. I was made. I remade myself. And I made in turn. I don't have the sensation of having begun to live. This is probably because I wouldn't want to die. People call me by my name, they send me letters and I answer. I feel deep friendship for a few human beings whom chance has enabled me to meet. To love. They write to me, I reply. We see one another from time to time, less and less often. And I write. For thirty years now I've had this habit, and it's had me. I shat in my pants when Gide received me at his home, rue Vaneau.* A century ago. The shit has dried. I write, I'm published. I'm even told that what I write doesn't dishonour me. I should be overjoyed. I am. What annoys me is that I'm going to have to die one of these days. Or evenings. This bothers me. Because I'll be caught off guard, without having lived. Because centuries wouldn't suffice for that. I've done nearly all the deeds that a normal man feels capable of doing. I've known men and women. Everything remains to be known. I've travelled a little. Everything remains to be seen. I find myself intelligent only in fits and starts; with such resources, I live with others but not with myself. My ignorance, my stupidity, is total. I'm not responsible for anything in regard to others once I feel tired. Physically. The heart roving left and right. The head tying knots. Wishing to hide myself away. To avoid the risk of meeting anyone at all. However, I need others, their warmth. But from afar. Afar. After a certain age, it's no longer life that we secrete. But rather death. The problem is not to die too unjustly.

✤

Our ability to love is limited. We know many more individuals than we're capable of loving, and this is rather what society is like. As if it were necessary to disperse, or to share out in thirty pieces, what we can give to only one person. Love removes a man from nearly all his friends.

✤

One speaks about workers, never about typists. Yet if there's something that surpasses a factory in horror, it's indeed an *office*.

✤

All the clocks in town ring out the hour one after the other.

✣

Paintings made of air. The paintings are no longer a part of the furniture but, rather, of space. Fragments of an absolute world hanging on a wall that is itself in the wind.

✣

The less I lie, the more I blush.

✣

Those who ask what you're writing because ... Those who ask nothing. They're afraid to know the answer.

Then there are our writer-friends. I knew one once who was already a little famous. He was always asking me what I was up to. If I were going to publish something, some day. Well, one morning, at his home, I told him that the wait was over, that I had lost my virginity in a review,* that I had done—and that others had done—what was necessary. *He didn't hear me.* At the beginning of my sentence, as if by intuition, he'd picked up a newspaper and as I was spieling out my miserable words, he kept acting distracted by something, putting down his rag only to ask me what I'd just said. I picked up my beret and left. No, this wasn't childishness. Nor persecution. If you had the time, I could cite several similar cases. So where's the meanness in such behaviour? Nowhere. How can it be explained? I've given up. We're perhaps incapable of loving each other a little, except in regard to a certain unhappy condition which, for that very reason, makes love doubtful. (Between men.)

✣

To be in error.

Good writers never are.

The others cannot help but be so.

There are mediocre writers whom we forget.

And the sublime ones whom we don't read yet who enchant our lives when, indeed, the error becomes more pronounced. (Pascal, Kierkegaard, Hölderlin.)

✣

What's annoying about a famous person is that he takes himself for what he's become, not for what he's remained.

✣

Dreams remember dreams.

✣

Without literature, we wouldn't know what a man thinks when he's alone.

✣

I prefer the other man's freedom to my own. So he'll let me be free.

✣

Behind closed yeses.*

✣

We seek to recall the last words of a dead man. We await the next words of a living person. We rarely listen.

✣

Some days I wonder how others manage to recognize me in the street. I go out for a stroll in a grasshopper's body, hardly walking at all. And here come people saying hello to me, what's worse, stopping me short, shaking my hand as if I still had one, asking me about my wife, my children, my work. Although I make off with a quick see-you-later, the rest of the day is done for. The grasshopper will find itself feeling better.

✣

He gave himself his own autographs.

✣

We write because we're like everyone and everyone resembles no one.

✢

In order for others to have confidence in us, we first need to let ourselves be robbed by them without our saying anything.

✢

My only and insane form of misogyny—I don't forgive women for loving men.

✢

They're worming verses out of my heart.

✢

Caskets are nailed shut as if we're afraid the corpses will fly off.

✢

What I write is to be read in a train by a bored traveller who finds one of my books, forgotten, on a seat.

✢

Fragments of truth. It's when we believe we're telling the whole truth that we run the risk of bringing out the fragment. If we think 'fragment', we totalize nothingness.

✤

Woman is the body of man.*

✤

The impossibility of remaining alone with a child. I'm afraid.

✤

Death employs us as the travelling salesmen of its business. We *deliver* its goods. Then it dismisses us. After a well- or ill-accomplished mission. With a medal or a reprimand. *Vive la frousse. La Frouce.**

✤

Writing is *physical*.

✤

Time. While I'm writing, a captured tiger turns itself into a bird and flies off. I'll have to begin all over again.

✤

A writer is always merely the ghostwriter of the child who's already seen everything.

✤

All of Racine's characters have earned their high-school diplomas.

✤

It's not in order to be read that you write. It's in order to be experienced, a little.

✤

And if no one is left, I'll be that one (God).

✤

Man is man's dream.

✤

Everything I find myself able to do I find insignificant.

✤

Certain that when I die I'll scream that it's unjust, that if I had known it was for good I'd have paid even less attention.

✤

I can't manage to believe that I'm the only one who pisses, and so on. That I'm the only one who's totally idiotic, or totally absent from the world for quite a few hours every day. So I read, seeking in the writing of others, or in colloquial speech, what will allow me not to believe I'm the absolute only one who . . . Who does what? The work hides the man, so be it. How I wish it'd strip off his clothes! For ultimately we know everything. What is essential would be in the work only if *everything* were found there. But this is not the case.

✣

What I'd in fact be interested in knowing is what kills a man before he walks onto the stage, and the confirmation of this murder. Einstein saying: If I could live my life over again, I'd be a plumber.*

✣

There's only one thing to do—be in love. To run the risk of being in love. Otherwise, you're dead.

✣

Writing is saying something to someone who's not there. Who'll never be there. Or if he's there, we'll be the ones who've gone away.

✣

Poets are ruminants.

✣

Silence is like a block of ice melted by words.

✣

The time you spend writing is wasted for what you seek by means of writing. (How merry!)

✣

A dream. Becoming the son of one's children. I thought of that a while ago as I was watching some men playing cards. As I pondered those fat gentlemen, I told myself that my children will perhaps belong to that strange race one day. But that I'll have long been chewing dandelions in my funereal cradle.

✣

To have a destiny, how stupid! It's liberating oneself from all destinies that matters a little.

✣

What's abstract is man before God, and lost in Him.

✣

What atheists lack is a belief in God. And vice versa. This is the mess we're in.

✣

Gide believed in God through his wife.* It's surer that way.

✣

Living means taking an oral examination.

✛

When we meet a man, we play a game of life with him. He plays or doesn't play. If he doesn't play, we pick up our chips of presence or, rather, absence, and we go back home. Back inside ourselves. But there's a rub. The chips are excited, unhappy, we need to amuse them. The mind starts bubbling. We write.

✛

He'd shout 'God is dead!' while stuffing his fingers in his ears.

✛

I write when I sense I'm detouring through myself.

✛

We write because no one listens.

✛

He liked himself a lot. He'd say excuse me to himself whenever he burped.

✛

I've made a no for myself.

✛

Literature is not everything when it becomes every-thing for a human being. It's everything when he could do without it.

✣

'The being of literature is nothing but its technique.'* So be it. What's strange is that you need to be at least Kafka before this certainty appears. We could say that, for a given acute sensibility, an equally acute technique.

✣

PAPER COLLAGE 3

I can't imagine a man constantly occupied only by what he's doing, has done, will do. No matter what he's doing. It's unthinkable for me that a man doesn't experience every day, if only for a quarter of an instant, the sentiment of emptiness, the thought that living is impossible. It's this quarter of an instant that fascinates me. It's fashioned my life. A quarter of an instant without the slightest reference, the slightest memory, the slightest heredity; that's neither cruel nor pessimistic; and that's imperceptible to others. A fleeting pain that passes through you like an aeroplane flying through a cloud. It's better to be alone when this happens. Really. For whatever you're doing at that moment, you indeed have a single wish—to follow the pain and consent to it. I'd experience this on the stage when I was given rather important roles. Between two lines of a dialogue, it'd start hitting me, but not nastily, for it didn't know what I was up to. Yet at that point my presence on the stage would be over. I'd immediately find myself in a world that was deadlocked, had come to a standstill, a sort of Grévin Wax Museum,* and that had been cast off—without actually being so—beyond the more or less interesting part that I was acting. A state of absolute absurdity. If only the theatre were at stake! All this continues in the remotest possible places. There, at least, I'm able to travel, undisturbed, on the wings of this pain—oh, call it a daily tingling that permeates every instant, one after another, without establishing a *chronology*, of what it thinks my life is.

❖

It's wrong to complain. If we knew where we came from, where we are and where we're going, it would be absolute hell.

❖

We ask for our daily crumb of love. We're given a ton for eternity, which is death.

❖

Man has himself awakened by a porter who's stayed up all night for him.

❖

It's when I'm alone that I feel the most human. How to reconcile this state with that other one when time is spent with another person? I try. It's difficult. It'd be better for one who has known an inebriated solitude—I don't mean drinking—not to marry, not to spend time with anyone else. He knows where his loves are. And his disasters. They can't be deposited anywhere. As human beings, we're fit for the garbage bin. Everything that makes us live ends up in one.

❖

When you know the wings of the theatre well, you don't want to sit in the audience. Even less act on the stage. Where to, then?

✦

Getting yourself elected by someone who's not yourself is ridiculous. Even more ridiculous.

✦

Death's self-publishing costs.

✦

Once there's circulation, there's lyricism. There's nothing more lyrical than blood. Whence, perhaps, one lyricism per person. A special heartbeat that strikes the hour of discourse that's uninterrupted because it's discontinuous.

✦

I can only envy those artists so permeated by time that a construction site is established and opens out in front of them. *Work* becomes possible, thereafter enabling them to be occupied as a carpenter, a mason, a woodcutter and the like know how to be.

What's enviable is this metamorphosis of artistry into craft.

Yet as to . . . inspiration? A word difficult to pronounce and impossible to *translate* because it covers no content. The very fact of working nullifies it.

❖

I write. It's not my trade. No trade resembles man. It's what I can do. I know that if I'm not writing, something is not quite right and announces a catastrophe. I have friends who are crazier than I am. As a young man, I was also crazy. When I hadn't turned out my daily ten pages of nonsense, I'd get sick. Or fall in love. Which amounts to the same thing. Now, it's different. I've consorted with others. Writing no longer seems tragic to me. On the contrary. There's worse. I believe writing is a privilege. A privilege for a poor man.

❖

A quill is the sharpest thing I've found for boring through a minute's wall, for breaking the poisoned sequence of time. Yet what if the wall receded as I headed for it, at the same speed? What if we were digging only distance?

❖

I invent as I go along, claims the novelist. Yet words are contagious. And every book is sick, though rarely contagious. However, a good book, a beautiful book, passes its sickness on to us. To the extent that it dies from it.

✛

There's always something unreadable in a poem (worthy of the name). What's unreadable is the poem itself, which has been made equivalent to nature. It can't be harvested. We protect our hands with gloves when we *sow*.

✛

Writing passes time.

Music gets time to pass.

Painting effaces it.

✛

Whoever writes to save himself is already doomed.

✛

It's not because you visit a cemetery that you know its inhabitants.

✛

Reading: The resurrection of Lazarus. Lifting the slab off the tomb of words.

✛

He was weeping with cold tears.

✣

Reaching the point where you can't tell the truth any more about who you really are. It's too unbearable. Unhearable. Indecent. Worse than making love in the street.

✣

You don't need to be a great literary scholar to know how rare it is to be truly focused on what the words written on a blank sheet of paper are trying . . . to drink, to wash away, as it were, aiming at a broader, more open life. Word-*prows* testing waters you know are mined. So what, then, if you explode with them? How very rare! We use words so we won't need them any more. But nothing sprouts back faster than a word.

✣

I'm more sensitive to others when I think of them than when I see them. Everything that ensues . . . Love is difficult.

✣

It's easier to do too much than just enough. But according to what criterion?

✣

It's a little as if death were waiting for us in the staircase and you had to find fast what your memory of life will be for the eternity you'll spend beneath the board.

❖

If you have to fall into the water in order to see if your friend will come and pull you out, well . . .

❖

Human gestures flattened out against the quivering air—against quivering reality, like the shadow of a man on a Hiroshima pavement.* The distance between the graffiti and the trace of someone's passing is reduced at night, when all tasks have ceased and every desire has slipped into a welcome weariness. At this point an extended hand, a shared cigarette—and the world opens once again, deducted from the original nothingness.

❖

To make a success of one's life—Rimbaud.

To succeed in life—nearly everyone!

❖

The vulnerability of poems. For ever intact.

❖

With whom, with what, keep a souvenir of life?

✣

'Ah, if I had the time, if I had the time!' What time?

✣

The smile's mouse-hole.

✣

The opposite of illness is not health. It's another illness.

✣

We can't eternally criticize what we love with the excuse that others—who are unworthy—also love it. This is one of the decimals of the modern intellect.

✣

A poem hides something obvious. Like a woman, her sexual organs. (Less and less often.) Hence the necessity of getting a poem to like you so it'll offer itself to you. Open itself up. Let itself be unfolded. Undone. Dress it as you undress it. What more beautiful garment than skin?

✣

Writing suffices unto itself only when it's mediocre, utilitarian. Otherwise, it designates a point. A needle in a haystack. Of sound.

✤

How one is alone living alone!

✤

A poem—a wild animal of language. Let it live free. Risk dying. Our dying.

✤

Aren't we destined to be with others in good as in evil? And doesn't love decree solitude? The same kind of solitude that leads to love?

✤

What I'm trying to say time and again is very simple. There's something, every day, that interrupts the social, emotional or intellectual adventure and leaves a guy in the lurch, stunned—whoever he is and whatever he's doing. He has to put his boots back on.

✤

One of the most ludicrous ideas that human beings have come up with is surely that of attributing fame, erecting statues and awarding medals to one another.

When did they first start going off their rocker in this way? What detective novel will give us the motive and the scene of the crime? The culprit?

❖

To live because of something other than that which gave the opportunity to a man and a woman to fling themselves upon each other.

❖

What I've learnt is that it's more difficult to write simply than hermetically. What's hermetic needs to be absorbed by what's simple. Hölderlin knew this, as did Artaud.

❖

I've never intended to lock myself up in literature, but, rather, to confront what little of it I have in the blood with the daily risks of getting rid of it. (All the while wishing, perhaps, that a little of the little remains!)

❖

Look at me—in absolute brotherhood with animals, Nature, the speechless world.

❖

Whoever sees God once moves no more.

✛

Once we've learnt the answer, we often say: That's what I thought. Thinking is perhaps this.

✛

Far into the night of the body, spoken words have died . . .

✛

However you sort it out, literature is the habitat of solitude. Desire. Impatience.

✛

We're not all as intelligent. But all as stupid. As sensitive!

✛

Nothing appears so rarely as what is natural.

✛

Writing is no proof of brotherhood. Why would it be one? Why would writing, painting and so on make one better? What makes one better? Poverty?

✛

I'd be able to get along only with a man who admitted that he'd felt the desire to kill himself and that this desire persisted—like a fire in a hearth. A man who had *understood*, known, experienced what's impossible and used this knowledge for living, beyond all optimism, etc. An emancipated man. This is rare.

✤

I read newspapers. I *keep myself in the flow*. I listen to the radio. I read my contemporaries, even those who will be read only by me—and there are lots of them, believe me! So what I could miss out on is the 'atmosphere', two or three conversations in a cafe. Where are the margins found? Living in seclusion? From what? From whom? People speak about the Pompidou Centre. They say: 'You need to have seen this, heard that . . .' No, you don't. Either the energy exists or it doesn't. It matters little whether you're on an island, in a prison or in a hospital. What's serious is exile. Leaving your irrational loves. I feel sorry for the Russians who are deported from their country. A Russian tree doesn't look like a Swiss or American tree. Yes, it must be hard not to be able to speak your language in the street, in order to buy some bread. You chew the 'little that remains'.

✤

Poetry hides behind words. Whatever hides isn't absent. Yet it's another kind of presence, that of jealousy.

✣

A modern problem. It takes time. A construction site rather than a concert piece. Archaeology.

✣

Life being what it is, I don't see why one would falsify the duration by choosing to *act out the comedy,* never ceasing to be someone else, to lend one's body, one's sensibility, one's organs to fiction, whereas the raw fact of being alive, of being a man or a woman, already resembles nothing.

✣

The time has truly come to stop progress. We think of 'scientists' as if they were turbulent children: 'What kind of mischief will they get into next?' How true. But the worst has been done. Without the help of any god, all by ourselves, we can blow up the whole place.

✣

We're not modern because we use new processes—particularly in music—but, rather, because we wouldn't be able to express ourselves without them.

✢

It's obvious that the success of whiteness (a white sale!), that is a blank sheet of paper with only few words on it, certainly suited not a few candidates at the poetry fair who were wondering how to get their goods cleared through Customs.

✢

Thinking is remorse. But about what?

✢

How I'd like to be taken for a dog, to be invited to spend an evening below a table, with people handing me a bone now and then.

✢

The present—a nest of memories! Life writes itself along. We hope ourselves along!

✢

How I'd like to meet someone who'd prevent me from preferring to die rather than to live with him!

✢

There's only one language to translate—one's own. Keep references at bay as long as possible. Find words that cut across.

✣

Looking at a living person as we'll *see him again* when we learn he's died. Difficult.

✣

The emotion can be identified at the place that prompts its appearance.

✣

Living with a loved one who's dead. A poem is this, with words.

✣

Living gets me drunk.

✣

The sower's gesture. And the sower of gestures.

✣

It'd suffice to write without publishing—without wanting to publish—to keep your mind at rest. This is like saying it'd suffice to be unborn. For not only ambition is at stake. Pride. Breathing also remains mysterious. Air.

❖

Being good, indeed. With whom? Who's going to bear my goodness? Here, doggie.

❖

History. Why have I never witnessed a great event? I learnt why later. I was told that I was there.

❖

Those people whose word changes every day. Like today's special. Listening to them is like reading a newspaper.

❖

Anyone is capable of writing anything by *claiming to represent* poetry.

❖

I'm convinced you meet up with your death during your lifetime. But you don't recognize it. You hardly run the risk of feeling a shiver. Often in someone else's gaze.

❖

We don't make mistakes. We change.

✣

Writing to an old friend or an old mistress from the past. It's absurd. It's all over. The unforgettable coitus of friendship is as unforgiving as the other one. It's really all over.

✣

A poem is made to be read; a woman, to be caressed. An old bachelor poem doesn't exist.

✣

Don't take her crabs for her beaver.

✣

Love is the dependence of independence.

✣

Modern music—more for playing, for interpreting, than for listening.

✣

Another person is like a distant province.*

✣

Neologisms are loincloths.

✣

Human beings look at one another as if they've never seen one another. With animals, it's the opposite.

✤

For years now I've no longer touched the woman who's brave enough to live with me. This doesn't prevent me from loving her. It prevents me from touching another woman.

✤

Our world will perhaps be the stage of a great confirmation—human beings aren't made for loving their neighbour as themselves, despite the well-known watchword. Yet they need to help one another survive—without love.

✤

Difficult to live in a world where lovers don't dare to avow their love—their loves—until they've become *successful* in the society in which they've tried to make all love disgusting.

✤

Loving literature means being convinced there's always a written sentence that will renew our taste for life, so often diminished after we've listened to human beings for too long. To ourselves, among others.

✤

We all die young.*

✛

That you have to love yourself a lot, indeed adore yourself, in order to put up with yourself a little, dooms all our relationships.

✛

Our posterity is the present.

✛

Human beings have seen enough of one another.

✛

I defy anyone to find anyone else funny for very long.

✛

The unpleasant sensation of being alive like an intruder. To occupy the territory of another person, whom I have killed.

✛

A glutton for laziness.

✛

Solitude, my smoking jacket.

✛

The dead ever more numerous behind us. And we're always the first and last people alive. Saturation.

❖

Nothing happens and when something happens, it's death.

❖

I'll have slept a lot on my feet while listening to what either I or the other person was saying . . .

❖

Racine is untranslatable because there's very little poetry in his plays. But make a messy translation of Sophocles or Shakespeare and something always remains—what's essential to every living human being, whoever he is and whatever he says or does.

❖

How many very bright human beings never manage to experience poetic phenomena because they think poets exist.

❖

We should read a poem only in Braille. With our fingertips.

❖

Have the first word.

✤

Their muse muzzles.

✤

Fear fosters competition.

✤

Free will. You decide when you're going to die. You wait. The countdown.

✤

A race to which one feels no pride in belonging between the ages of ten and eighty.

✤

While writing, I never have the impression of *rising*. Nor of descending. Instead, of showing up to disturb—even if only a little—an ill-established order that will modify—even if only a little—the shapes of a puzzle which, I hope, will reveal truth. Beyond metaphors, lyricism and so on. The naked truth.

✤

You take words for playthings only when it's all over with human beings. You play at being checkmated.

✤

To be the lover of a farm girl, a simple cafe waitress or a factory worker, who comes home tuckered out in the evening. You've prepared her dinner. You softly caress her. Is this impossible?

✤

Humour depends not on language but, rather, on the space in which you dip it. Compromise it. Gut it.

✤

Don't pay attention on purpose.

✤

The bridge. Don't touch the railing. But it's there. Otherwise, dizziness.

✤

He was more intelligent than his own average.

✤

Little else besides nakedness fascinates me, but it's still too dressed up. It's difficult to explain to an undressed woman that she's still not naked enough.

✤

How can you expect to learn what I do when I'm alone, as long as you're here?

✤

Man tells himself a story that's not his.

✣

Real flowers wither. Looking ahead to other flowers. Artificial flowers wither he who makes them.

✣

Painting blocks vision in order to better receive the invisible.

✣

It'd be good if we could love one another without loving one another.

✣

We capitalists of speech dream of comprehending one another, of getting to know one another, without words. Through gestures. One always hears—how marvellous to understand one another without having to speak. But the silence of a human being who can't speak is quickly unbearable.

✣

It took me only forty years to get by without other people, to stop being nice to them merely so they'd be nice to me. Have pity. To live beneath the sky of nothingness. Neither war nor love.

✣

The best readers are those who are jealous of manuscripts.

✤

Stupidity begins to make sense only when it's clarified by a mind that chases after it. Instead of asking it for help.

✤

Men of *authority*. Who dare to say: 'I like X a lot. I believe in him. He'll be successful.' This is the problem. (If I let myself develop the argument, I'd be one, too.)

✤

Any new element in human doings makes a stir, changes the *overall picture*. A word can live with a word, and change its fate.

✤

Life is monotonous, the monotony broken by the death of people we love, by friendship or by love. But the word has nothing pejorative about it. My hours follow my kids' schedule. When they go to school, I come to work.

✤

I've not left Paris. No reason to do so. I simply pre-
ferred Brittany. Betting I'd not Paris-h there—no
pun intended! Not really knowing whether I wouldn't
break my back and go bust. I started going there
gradually. At first for six months every year, fall and
winter, all alone, to Saint-Malo—a perfectly sinister
town, probably because of its inhabitants.* I like
streets and street life too much to have stayed there
for ever. Here in the Finistère, it's the opposite. You
have the impression of entering a big family. Every-
thing takes place in the streets, in the cafes, that is,
everything that interests me: what I expect of others,
those thousand and one trifles that make up the
ongoing psychoanalysis of human beings. *Private
life* doesn't seem to exist. This is false, of course. Yet
at least everyone knows the streets exist. People you
never see in the streets—and there are some—could
just as well live elsewhere. Streets are special. A way
of living with everyone and no one. You recognize a
man of the streets by the way he walks. Fishermen
are unforgettable *walkers*.

✤

Writing is a cheerful activity. You can cheerfully
write that you're going to kill yourself. Writing can
aim only for an ellipse, a poem or the illusion of
efficiency. Language is an ocean of words. As for
me, either I almost drown in it or, when the tide

goes out, I look around, walking on what's left behind. Holes, puddles. Fragmentary writing means these puddles, these marine remnants, these shells, these wet pieces of evidence. My attentiveness dries them off. The opposite of continuous discourse, which is life, between nothingness and what is palpable. Like Tom Thumb, except that the pebbles are in front of me. How to read these scraps? There's a time, a moment, for reading the newspaper, for reading a novel or a poem. But notes? Beyond the note there is—there's only—the solitary inveterate aphorism. Cold strained words.

❖

Writing well is a meaningless notion. Today, you can hope only for a total rupture. This isn't easy. You mustn't do it intentionally, but rather live. What I like in a writer is what escapes him after he has done his eliminating. Literature makes sense only when it's monstrous. Writing is Balzac, Hugo, Proust. Dragnet fishermen gone mad.

❖

Evoking suicide exorcizes, as it were, the mortuary qualities dragged along by life before the appropriate flowers and wreaths. The first human beings didn't know they were going to die. We tend to know this too much. For me, poetry is the span of time during which man forgets he's going to die. An absence of time, if you will. This could explain Rimbaud, who probably had the impression he'd killed death. Which let him live. During his Ethiopian years, it was as if death had left him in the lurch, had forgotten him in turn.* By snatching all his gifts, all his jewels, it protected him from old age. Life debases. I think it's Henri de Régnier who declared this.* That's absurd. Life is everywhere. Wherever we are. We are life. This is why one mustn't feel on the fringes of society, or in seclusion. It's not *possible*.

✣

A poem has an inside and an outside, it's a thing at the heart of which you can dwell. And when the inside becomes too comfortable, allows the poet to strike a pose or even take a rest, you sense this right away. A poem belongs to the world and fits into all that's invisible, into all that's elsewhere, into what Bonnefoy calls the hinterland.* Things take place inside us, go through us, give us a workout, even as one says the sea is worked up, without our being their masters. Or their slaves. The subject matter ignores us, couldn't care less about us. Take it or leave it. Art is merely the difficult retrieval of these signs that slip away from the most elementary daily life, even as the whole remains beyond any detail belonging to it. Thus, during sleep, I don't know what keeps watch, what drifts to the bottom—the bottle is no longer shaken. What one says is interesting only if uttered at the borders of this absence from the diurnal world. Absence is not the exact word. Shadow gives meaning, another meaning, to light.

✜

The quality in the quantity, without getting mixed up!

✜

Saying 'I' is incomparably more modest than saying 'we'. This should be obvious. But it isn't, they say.

✜

Begging forgiveness because you've done nothing wrong.

✜

When you have character, you don't need it. (This suits everyone.)

✜

He's considered to be a genius, every three weeks, by different people.

✣

Many politicians are failed writers.* Many writers are failed politicians. This is easy to perceive. Read. Listen.

✣

Attain the point where there's no sense in committing suicide. 'A pistol is a little stupid.'*

✣

Brittany. Weather is more present here than elsewhere because of the stone, the water, the sky. A magical, more than historical weather to the extent that it discourages all meteorological theories. I often hear it authoritatively stated on the radio that it's raining in Brittany. As soon said, and look at the blue sky! This resembles us.

✣

In the wings, you know if a play is good.

✣

A poet has only Time for, with, him.

✣

A sense of modesty is saying everything, showing everything and there's still something left over.

✤

Human beings are old babies.

✤

You need character only two or three times during your lifetime.

✤

We perhaps come from something more than from someone.

✤

What good is a key if there's no lock?

✤

A poet's words make what they stalk appear—and flee. The archer is vanquished, but his words are aware of the 'other side'.

✤

One is never satisfied. Stendhal dreamt of being Molière and would go to the Comédie Française, a copy of *The Miser* in hand, in order to underline passages where the audience laughed.* Just to get the recipe. He failed. Miserably. Like Baudelaire. Like Balzac. Poor Stendhal. He was only able to write *The Chartreuse of Parma.*

✣

It's always too late when we meet the human beings we love. They no longer want any more love. Or it's too early. All they want is love. Never during. At the right time.

✣

I don't see why I shouldn't write about my wife, my children, my dog. The problem is only that I don't write well enough about them. I don't write at the point where their poetry emerges. Don't come and tell me that poetry lies outside our experience of time. That it's a sort of luxury. If I'm neither Mallarmé nor Hölderlin nor Hopkins, this isn't because I can't recognize their constant metamorphosis. I probably lack the genius that manages to energize our marvel at existing. We're among ourselves during our respective lifetimes. We're with one another, beyond the mere anecdote of existing. I've tried to live accordingly, thanks to my innermost laws. An energy that's made me neither more nor less efficient as far as my language goes. Yet that's perhaps made me more sensitive to the language of other people. I've scoured off the ivory of my tower down to what is sensitive in everyday life.

✤

Poetry is everywhere. Everywhere except in language. Break open language, clear it through Customs, instead of squeezing into its corset.

✤

A poet is one who accepts to be the attentive slave of what goes beyond him.

✤

Sex has no sex.

✤

It's completely obvious that writing *looks out on* something other than mankind, since people continue to write despite their success or failure.

✤

A human being speaks, but like a blind man walking through a field of daisies. Trampling everything unknowingly. Speech is the best-shared thing in the world. But also the most unrecognized. If everyone were rich, money would lose its meaning.

✤

A poem catches all the illnesses. Acts as a guinea pig. In order to save everyday language.

✛

We speak, we even write, at a great distance from a place of which we have an idea now and then. But it's not really an idea. Like a shiver of Being, a memory from before our own existence, before everything. This shiver decrees what's immeasurable. No discourse can cover it, yet a few white-hot 'isolated' words risk establishing the limits of the land registry.

✛

Intuition about a place where words would go to get their health back. Far from where people cogitate, agitate, prophesize, 'profesize', decide, conclude. Far from discourse.

✛

Writing while avoiding to speak about what happens to us every day is like walking on the eggs of language. They can be beautiful, I won't say the contrary. But I can refuse to look at them. To look only at them. They have to tell me what they've got inside. A tree is a tree. Rich, alive. But I can't allow myself to sleep on one of its branches. I have to sleep. And while I sleep, the tree stays outdoors. It doesn't bother itself with coming and finding me. Waking me. I'm the one who'll return tomorrow and see it. Oh, it'll still be there, sampling its roots, gobbling down its leaves. Perhaps I'll start speaking about it again, thinking I'm speaking about something else. But ultimately, no, that's not possible. Shit on the tree. And leaving it behind, I'll meet up with a wild rose, a violet, or—why not?—a dead leaf. Hey, what's this? Thank you. Thank you very much. And I'll take them to my room. A tree is a little cumbersome. But a violet, a butterfly or God knows what (and He wants to know nothing), all right. On top of this, the neighbour will have his wife who's broken her leg during the day. We never say hello to each other. We don't like each other. But now I'll need to help him transport his wife to the hospital, find a taxi. So someone knocks on the door. One of my kids goes to open it. I hear some vague noises, some words colliding. I get up. 'Monsieur Verdelin's here and doesn't know how to get his wife to the hospital. Go and help him.'* Me, who thought I was going to spend a nice evening with my violet, my butterfly. That damned Verdelin! I arrive. Ev'ning, ev'ning. We're still not speaking much to each other, but it's not the same. All right, let's go to the hospital.

✣

Poetry is on the night's agenda.

✣

Fully describing the slightest moment of any person's life—yours, mine—would necessitate thousands of pages, indeed thousands of moments of writing time during which all the other, similar, slight moments would be neglected. This is the drama of a writer in his purest state. As his *oeuvre* progresses, a delay sets in that can never be overcome. Life can't be transcribed in its cruel permanence, its continuity. All one can do is set sail in it. Have a hearty appetite. Yet this needs to be reinitiated time and again *in aeternum*.

✣

Words conceal a text even as actors conceal a play.

✣

Eyes pop out of a man at the worst moments. Eyes are human oysters. A man who knows his eyes are glassy—he got drunk the night before—puts on a pair of sunglasses. There's a world of difference between those who wear glasses and those who don't. Eyes are like nakedness. They give and receive. Nothing is more moving, or disastrous, than a *look*. Eyes are the true sexual organs of a human being. Or rather, of any living being. Fish, seagulls, dogs and cats have unforgettable looks. But there are no glasses for animals to wear.

✣

Strange that one speaks of childhood only after childhood. Of adulthood, perhaps, this happens during death.

✣

Time's time.

✣

The response is neither outside nor inside the text. It's *the* text.

✣

We get drunk in order to rise to the heights of others' indifference.

✣

The poet both makes and climbs over the wall of language.

✣

In poetry, the poem is the least thing.

✣

I live as if I had been.

✢

Life is every now and then.

✢

Poetry is truth. Whence superstition. Or wagering. Risk.

✢

Poetic speech is the concentration camp of language. Deported speech.

✢

Inventing gods meant decongesting what's mortal about mankind. The field of the possible was narrowed. Whence the degradation into the absurd, which is an imitation. Today, we need to start from the impossible. Whatever man does, the impossible exists. The unthinkable.

✢

You need to get involved in yourself. Just to see. You see.

✢

Speaking in the desert. Literature—withheld speech. Crushed speech. Discourse is damnation. No way around it. Wanting to do without, means swearing the end of humanity. Which does not touch the aphorism.

✛

There can be too much speech. What's essential is missing. A writer bungles his project by writing.

✛

Solitude was once romantic. It's become social. A fellow sitting alone in a cafe listens to the bullshit spoken at the next table. Eroticism, too. A couple arrives. How awful.

✛

Speech that dreams do not recover. It's the same speech. No obstacle. Speaking to oneself in time.

Love in danger.

Speech that doesn't know what we know. That's neither heard nor learnt anything. That never speaks up. Inhabited solitude. Haunted solitude.

✛

Stammering when you're spoken to in your own language.

✤

Life dies now and then. We outlive it.

✤

The speech *shore*.

The tide.

More or less.

If we didn't know there are rocks, at high tide?

Literature—the sea of writing.

No tourists.

✤

Words that open like oysters.

✤

The problem—we imagine things. Poetry is the opposite. A poetry from nowhere, from anywhere, from everywhere.

✤

Outdoors speech. Wandering.

✤

The impossibility of lying. Yet for all that, to not tell the truth.

✛

Either literature is what remains when we've left the company of other human beings, in the evening, or in the morning before meeting up with them again. Or it's the risk of lost words during the day.

✛

Something recognizable. You turn on the radio. After two seconds, you know what it's all about. The oral layer is almost immediately spotted. And in daily life you almost always know who you're doing business with, as one says. It's extremely rare when we don't need to change gears, to interrupt the perpetual speech inside us. Friendship is when the two kinds of speech emerge, travel side by side, the words of one around the shoulders of the other.

✛

Getting the message through. Getting the writing through. The Pony Express.

✛

Sartre—a vegetarian who likes only raw meat.*

✛

Solitude is noticing others' solitude.

✜

We've become very rich. The only bite to eat we have is poetry.

✜

To love or not to love, that is the question.

✜

Writing is not advancing but, rather, retreating in order to better blow the fuses of language.

✜

Between the 'you' and the fiction.

✜

Neither speaking well nor thinking right. Something else. On which saying and thinking depend.

✜

A poet—an unskilled worker of language. Once a joint gets wobbly and there's *play* in it, he repairs, readjusts. An endless task.

✜

We can share only solitude. Place your bets.

✤

Words shade sense.

✤

We bear everything—war, suffering, exile, etc. It's the passing from one state to another that's terrible. The time to get settled.

✤

Insanity and suffering cannot mimic themselves very long.

✤

Often, in fact, most of the time, what I write makes sense only if unpublished. Here's an example!

✤

How we can be mistaken—it's not the sea you hear in a shell but, rather, the ebb and flow of your blood.

✤

Words are masks that the poet adjusts on the thousand and one faces of reality so that it can go out and party without being recognized—and scoffed at—by those who think they are its owners.

✤

In the train. Across from me is a kid. He's more annoying than all the travellers put together. But he's a kid. Grim-looking, naughty and so on—like almost all kids. I was once one. Now I have three. I spend time with lots of kids. But all the same, this kid is less annoying, less unbearable than the guy next to me, who's reading . . .—I glimpse what, but the name of the paper escapes me—who is in any event reading, whatever it is, pure rubbish, judging merely by the illustrations. The kid is eating a *Lu* butter biscuit.* He's staring at me with enormous eyes because of the way his eyeglass lenses magnify them. I smile at him, he sticks out his tongue. His grandfather notices nothing. He's reading *Le Monde*, with one of those haughty airs that indicates that he has others. We're travelling between Redon and Vannes.*

✢

Do you know who wrote this? 'Africa is dark beneath too many sunrays. It's covered with what one could call the shadows of the sun.' Victor Hugo.

And this? 'When you see a man and remember his book, this is a bad sign.' And: 'When you read too fast and too softly, you hear nothing.' Blaise Pascal.

✢

Health is used for not dying every time you're seriously ill.

✜

What's evil is not what we think of others. It's what we think they think of us. Actually, they think nothing. Think nothing of us. So evil doesn't exist?

✜

Man is born good. The deterioration begins between the sixth and seventh months.

✜

What helps you to live isn't in life.

✜

Clocks vaunt Time.

✜

There's no one like everyone.

✜

In his day, everyone wrote music like Mozart. Except Mozart.

✜

There's worse than falling—the downward path. Those slutty *word*-tracks that cross our inner steppe, excluding all other kinds of language—then lights out. You're going to have to *forget* them, but it's impossible. They're indelible. You won't be able to avoid this rut any more, you'll have to go through it. I think every man, whoever he is, wherever he comes from, whatever he does, has heard this sleigh dragged along by wild immortal animals from before the dawn of man. Mankind's illnesses, cancer and so on, *calm* the words. Allow them to take a breather, to get their breath back, to make a stopover for the winter in the igloo of their progress.

The worst that can happen to us is opting for death, not being able to do otherwise, everything now taking on a spectral, unreal appearance, everything in a total loss of body, factuality, like crumbling piecrust. What efforts are needed so you won't let it be known—if only by a gesture, an intonation—to your loved ones, whom it's also impossible for us to exclude, to save from this imperative that comes from elsewhere, but whom we won't meet up with again elsewhere. How to nail here down? To what wall?

Emerging from this state, *forgetting* for good, this is probably what living means. But from what night do we emerge, at birth?

✛

A man who writes is always anxious, worried. He left the gas valve open. But where?

✣

Solitude has meaning only when it's total. (Which could explain getting used to prison, an illness. Resignation.) Is supportable only when total. The problem is being alone without being entirely so (married, children, friends). The love you risk feeling for 'your own' doesn't prevent solitude which is like a habit already taken up in childhood.

✣

You have to be a genius in order to write. Otherwise, it's too well written.

✣

To versify. To write verse. A world of difference.

✣

There's only one moment that interests me in a human being, no matter who he is or what he does—it's when he finds himself alone, either on a park bench, or in the john, or on a hospital bed. And what he makes of this moment.

✣

I've never heard a fisherman say he loves the sea.

✣

To draw out what's human from a human being, you have to wait until he dies. Provided something is left over.

✣

A word brings another along with it. This is true. But there's better. A word opens a door through which goes the next one which closes the door in order to open another one. By the end of every literary work a labyrinth has thus been established; all kinds of circulating within it are allowed, if not recommended. There's no side from which the work can be taken—no designated sexual organ—and I'm not speaking only of works that are supposed to be labyrinths. But from what angle should you pick up and reread Pascal's *Thoughts*, for example? After how many readings, that is, forays into the instituted maze, do you find your way?

✣

The aphorism—intelligence vanquished, and happy to be so.

✣

Having genius is to write when you don't want to write. But instead want to live.

✣

First the blackboard. Then the white sheet of paper. And afterwards?

✣

Where to enter the cave without tricking the Customs officers, without handing over the goods, without being identified?

Passage from the fragment to the ellipsis.

How to write without falling into the rut of the beautiful, and so on? How to prevent words from giving birth to little children they will be proud of? . . . Where can your language be learnt, be grasped?

✣

I write in holes.

✣

What's horrible about politicians and cops is that they look as though they were made for the job.

✣

Whoever wants to be right every day misses the weekly truth.

✣

Time—the world bank.

✣

Great pleasure—immense pleasure—lies in being lucid, *sober*, clear-headed, fully here. Another pleasure in being drunk, crazy, dismasted, although still fully here as well. This sums up everything.

✣

It's animals that have an inner life.

✣

Never forget that humans sleep. Fortunately.

✣

Beware of stoves that heat only themselves.

✣

I write curled up like a rifle hammer.

✣

We age ourselves before we age.

✣

Literary acquaintances. You don't read a book you receive in the same way as one you buy.

✢

No man will make me believe in God. Me less than any other.

✢

With heart and fang.

✢

SO TO SPEAK

My writing is like blowing my nose. It's not writing. It makes for a pile that shouldn't be published. It's not a book. If need be, it could be discovered after I've kicked the bucket. The writings would be in a suitcase and somebody would say: 'Hey, let's see what's inside.' Posthumously. A little book would be published. Something of this nature. This being said, I caught the bug early. But I'm almost cured of it. Because writing is an illness and creates illusions. If you're a great writer, you spend your life at it; you launch yourself into it. Proust . . . well, all the big guys. As for me, I dip my foot in the water. I see if the water is warm or cold. But perhaps drops remain. I dry off rather slowly and, as long as it takes me to dry off, drops fall—more or less the equivalents of these notes. They have no literary posture, in the good sense of the term, and no form, but they can make me seem likeable to other people. My writing is really something else. That there are fellows who write like me and are published is always amusing because one says: 'Here's a guy who makes hard cider . . .' But I don't want to make hard cider. It's not hard cider, it's what's left over. It's amusing to read, I've no doubts about that, something between the newspaper and the *Farmer's Almanac*. It invites you into a private room, it's something others don't say, but if they don't say it, it's because they say it otherwise. And say it better. In this sense, I'm my own character. I don't share out the few thoughts I have among characters because I don't have enough thoughts. So I keep them for myself and gulp them down constantly. Which makes me believe I'm a likeable fellow. You can say I'm a nice guy. However, there's no relation between this and literature. Indeed, I know very well what I'm up to, and if I wrote a History of Literature, I'd perhaps set aside two lines that would be good.

✣

I took notes so I could write a book.

I lived so I could be a man.

Trying-on sessions. That continue.

I managed to change my 'nature'. To no longer have one. This is what I wanted. For having ideas, fore-seeing oneself, is nothing. But to sense yourself becoming, little by little, through strokes of misfor-tune, he whom you never believed you'd become, strikes me as the only possible euphoric state. That really matters to us. It's too easy to say you can't write for yourself. You only need to look at those who say so, happy to have found this obvious fact to lay their dishonesty to rest. (In fact, what is 'self'?)

✣

Yes, yes, I know, I'm exhausting. But so much more for myself than for others.

✢

Life accepted as it is puts us to sleep.

✢

I enter a cafe. I ask for a sandwich. Then for a carafe of wine. The lady who runs the place looks at me: 'He's a drinker, this little guy.' All right. After confirming my order—I swear I had to—she brings the carafe to my table. I've bought the newspaper. I read. A cat comes over, rubs against my calves, which begin to purr in turn. I let myself go more or less, thinking I won't be able to leave this cafe. I feel numb, the carafe has been swigged down, but I can still write— here's the proof. Write, yes, but get up, pay, leave— it's going to be difficult. I'll probably stagger a little. I live in these boondocks. I'll come back to this cafe, the only tobacconist's around here. I'll probably be entitled to a look as big as a carafe. Perhaps I'll ultimately no longer want to return. I'll go five kilometres to get my tobacco. Being free would thus imply being blind, deaf and dumb. Or rather, acting and living as if this were the case. Admit it, admit it— it's difficult.

✢

If I got married, I'd forget I had a wife the day after the wedding. It'd perhaps be better if I remained single.

✣

Drinking. What's boozing, if not a *liquid* manner of corresponding, thanks to wine, or alcohol, with our natural state which is unhappiness. We need to manage to be unhappy euphorically, superficially, in order to say everything would go very well without wine.

✣

People lie. The novel attempts to explain why. The theatre, how. Only poetry, very rarely, touches the veridical sky.

✣

Mental washing shrinks life.

✣

Covered with myths. The Greeks knew this so well they created them in order to avoid false myths.

✣

Someone who deals with you as if you were nothing—this is your wish—is lost.

✣

A fount of knowledge produces not very drinkable water.

✣

Writing means telling a truth life cannot bear. When you write to a friend you're unhappy, the person living with you doesn't know anything about it. Unhappiness is transformed into everyday words, moods, 'scenes'.

✣

Of mice and men—I had nothing to kill them with, so I tamed them.

✣

Saint-Malo. While eating dinner this evening, I thought it was high time I wrote in my diary. When I was younger, fifteen years old, I'd attack it boldly, without crossing out a word. Today it's different. I know the genre is disparaged. Only fools, romantics or social climbers now write diaries. Or schoolboys. I don't know which category I should put myself in. Already my pen hesitates. I grope for words. However, I was really happy when I made this resolution a little earlier. A little girl was playing cards at the next table and I was watching her. It was this scene, this girl, that prompted my daydreaming. She was charming. Lively, with dimples, and incredible nerve. She knew all the customers except me, and would go over to them, show them a card and ask: 'What are you thinking of?' They'd come up with an answer, she'd return to her game and then go elsewhere. It was all perfectly absurd. Except for her delightful face, she had a nervous little body hidden beneath a sweater and a pair of pants. (This is what's in fashion, even among the poor.) I was sitting all alone in my corner, exchanging glances with her big, rather ugly sister (I presume) who was serving tables. The little girl wanted to give me the bill, a touching gesture. After I'd asked her if she wanted to play cards with me, she said: 'Oh no, not this evening. I'm going to eat. But tomorrow, if you wish.' All right. Then tomorrow. And for sure, I'll come back to see her and have her ask me what I'm thinking. God knows what I'll answer! Do we know what we're thinking?

✣

We're forced to come back to literature. And philosophy is therefore necessarily an art. The highest art? This remains to be seen. When a philosopher puts no belts on his ideas, the reward is poetic. Saint Augustine is thus a poet, Pascal a poet, Kierkegaard a poet. The only philosopher of modern times—for the Greeks, they're all poets—who seems to have reduced to a minimum the *liquid* part is Descartes, but remember that what turned him into a master thinker was a revelation, and thus a poetic act.

✤

The mind dries out those who are dry.

✤

I can write only when I'm not thinking of myself. When I've become absent to myself. Because I hate myself. I've been crushed. In order to write, in a resonant way, I have to be caught off guard.

✤

There are a thousand ways to hide the holes. Only one way not to hide them—poetry.

✤

I made a place for myself in the shade.

✤

If I is an Other, I speak of the Other when I say I.*

If genuine life is absent, I speak of absence when I speak of my life.* Our life is what we imagine.

✤

We'd have to be rather strong not to love someone who doesn't love us. And nobody loves us.

✣

Words let the text go by; like flowers, the wind.

✣

Everything I write would be ridiculed if I managed to produce an *oeuvre* worthy of the name. It's quite surprising that a few people let me know that they read me. But why didn't I toss all those 'whims' into the waste-paper basket? Certainly a man imprudent enough to publish notes taken for a novel, his working notes, would lose all desire to write the novel. How many writers keep themselves from speaking even a little of what they're working on! Which implies that everything I write would have genuine meaning only if the pile were found after my death. In this series of unpaid pieces, vague desires, half-kept promises and rough drafts must surely lie a kind of excessive self-consciousness and a lack of honesty that are recognized by those who publish me, thinking that the literary world needs a little of everything. All genres. Yet in this instance, the genre consists of not having one. Every time that I take up with writing, I'm persuaded it's going to be the last time. That I'm finally going to fuck off and leave myself alone. This cruel game has been going on for almost thirty years. Cruel because everything happens too fast for me to *take advantage* of it. I write as if I were rushing from one train station to the other, with my arse on fire. Which means that I always arrive either too late or too early. But with no time for waiting, either.

✣

THE MAGIC SLATE

To the laryngectomized.

He's joking as he examines my throat with his mirror. Nothing, it's nothing, not even pharyngitis, a few red spots, no frog to fuss about.* Then, almost distractedly but probing deeper, he pales, turns livid. He stands up, staggers back to his desk, strikes it with his fist and utters 'Oh my God' often enough to rouse the Devil. Which seems to have happened. He falls back into his chair, grasps his head. I go over to him, sit down across from him and ask what the matter is. But I know everything already. Why I've come to see him. Dazed, distraught, sweating, he's staring at me.

'Is it serious?'

'Well, yes . . . We'll do a biopsy tomorrow morning at eight o'clock . . .'

Not another word. Above all, not the word that has just given a spectral look to this man, to me, to the icy examination room. In a trance, he accompanies me back to the door. See you tomorrow. In the street, I tell myself I'll need to chuck some junk out of my mental attic in order to make room for this new 'idea'!

What had prompted me to consult this specialist whom I knew a little because we had once vaguely argued in an art gallery? Was it merely because of this slight pain, as if made by a gimlet or a crab digging its hole? Wasn't it, instead, some kind of inkling, for intuitions are rarely good? A certainty? Simply for confirmation? To put my mind 'at rest'?

Every Thursday, in Brest, I had to walk in front of a clinic where big letters as bright as brass trumpets spelt out a fascinating word on the wall:*

COBALT

In order to chase the word away as if it were an intruder who had trespassed too far into an undefended off-limits area, I would play with it, undo it, break it down into anagrams, more or less: Tolbiac,* tobacco(!), balcony, Balto . . .* But every week I couldn't help but gaze once again at this gilded word which—though at the time I couldn't grasp very well why—suggested something to me, warning me in its gleaming way, attracting me towards it as if it wanted me to find a place for it among the familiar words I used daily, those reflecting my usual high standards.

It was time to go home. To tell my family(!) what was happening. As for me, I was relieved—foolishly. I'd long feared that they'd have some kind of accident or illness. Now I sensed that I'd myself taken on all such calamities, even death. And I'd have to convince myself that a kind of resistance that I had least expected was at stake. The best-guarded kind. What had remained intact. I had no idea what a hospital, an operating room and so on were like. What a journey!

Anaesthesia for the biopsy. The results two days later. Positive. X-ray. The epiglottis—the parade of new words begins—has been hit. Covered with a light layer of dust or down. But the larynx is intact, according to these gentlemen, who seem rather out of their depth. I'm going to be sent to Morlaix, to a super-specialist. He performs operations. Let's go. Yes, yes, a confirmation. No time to lose. And they're even going to be nice to me. Strings are going to be pulled—the expression this gentleman uses. I'll go to Paris for even more security. A man named L.,* the crack of the crack surgeons, will perform the operation. A ninety-five per cent success rate, my dear woman. (Already, no one is speaking to me any more.)

I tidy up my digs. If I kick the bucket, then I wouldn't want certain notebooks filled with stupidities to be found. A scavenger will later find them at the dump three miles from here, worry about what he reads and try to learn who the author is. He'll send me a letter: 'Dear Sir, It has taken me two months to dare to write to you. Up to a point, what had happened was ordinary. Like so many other people, I was emptying out my garbage bin at the P. dump—there is neither disgrace nor honour in such an act!—when I came across the notebooks making up your diary, bound by a rubber band. I saved them out of absolute respect for the Written Word, the same respect that makes me keep all my books, deluxe editions and paperbacks alike, no matter how bad or beautiful the writing is. The act of writing implies a secret glimmer, an unveiled hope, a confident giving over of oneself that commands respect. I therefore read—why would I have saved the notebooks otherwise?—your abandoned 'analysis notebooks'. I was quivering with indiscreetness when I did so, torn between my desire to keep reading and an acute awareness of my shameful curiosity. It was an excuse that I was seeking. Already in the act of picking up the notebooks, and even more so in the looking around beforehand that had enabled me to spot them, everything was told. How true it is that we notice only what interests us. So I secretly continued reading, my heart beating, for that is how things should be appreciated—for themselves, not because celebrities were involved. Your emotions, your doubts and your hopes in the 1940s were (and still are!) so similar to mine that it seemed both necessary and decisive for me to learn how everything had turned out. Had 'The Indifferent Man' been born? Had your study of Valéry appeared? And your essays on Stendhal, Voltaire and all the others? What a lesson for someone like me, whose poetic universe had until then consisted only of Jean Richepin, Jehan Rictus and Georges Fourest!* While reading your diary, I patiently waited for two months before softly pronouncing your name. Ah, why hadn't I done so earlier?! . . . Perros, indeed, that odd fellow with his motorcycle, his cap, his pipe . . . And what enchanted me especially was your pipe, as in your diary whenever you record feelings of satisfaction in the evening . . . So Georges Perros, the guy who would write to Gide and somersault with joy when the mentor replied, lived nearby. If you can forgive me for this "rape" of your private life, allow me to write to you from time to time . . .'

Then we met. But alas, I couldn't utter a word to him. They had cut out my vocal cords.

The surgeon in Morlaix: 'A mouth is disgusting.'

It's true I feared for my wife and kids. And prefer this has happened to me, for I don't need courage—

a luxury. No, it's something else. Harsher. More absolute. That you never need. Yet that's there. The poor man's hidden savings. To be opened only in an emergency. This is where we are.

Some friends worry about the quality of the surgeon who's going to operate on me. They go into action. The latest news, after checking—telephone calls to friends, to friends of friends and so on—is that he's in fact very good. Well, all the better. Let's go to him, then. It's odd to think one surgeon is superior to another. But this also must be true.

Paris. L. Hospital.* The great entrance hall, with its . . . reception, has a French Revolution look to it. Sentry boxes, black grimy walls, poor people in line. Get in line. And they're quick with the question: 'Whom should we contact in case . . .' It's reassuring. But because the questioner spends her whole day at such tasks, there's no way I can joke a little. Not even a little. This is one aspect of the situation. You get caught up in a system in which your own words are excluded. Shut up, or get yourself treated elsewhere. You're taking someone else's place. Which is still warm. As long as it takes to change the sheets. Only one bed was free that day. 'Consider yourself lucky.' All the same, she adds: 'in your misfortune!'

Thank you, ma'am. A strange change for a man with no idea of what slippers and pyjamas are . . . But my name is sewn on everything—socks, shirts, underpants, everything. No way to locate yourself in such a mess.

It's becoming serious. The IV drips have exhausted me. The crack of the crack surgeons—he looks like a gentle rugby player, and he surely comes from southwestern France—hesitates between a 'partial' and a 'total'(???), rummages about in my throat with two fingers of his rubber-gloved hand, muttering a few 'it's damned annoying's that go straight to my heart. The fellow's not very talkative, but it's true I've nothing to teach him. I let myself be manipulated as if I were a sack. An obsession with sacks. With being a sack. An absolute loss of all personality—so long as . . .—of all presence, of all that nonsense that's ultimately just for socializing, pride, dignity . . . Get me out of here, if possible, and we'll see about all that later. Extremely touchy, I sense the animal nibbling my body, my 'innerness'. I show my throat and my buttocks, my arm and my neck, to whoever wants to see them. Needles are stuck into me more or less everywhere—hey, you want another one, here you go. A body in transit.

Shots, blood tests, IV drips. They're often done slop-pily. To the extent I almost faint. Wimp! Manlette! My pale body like an aspirin pill! My birdlike wrists! (Laughter in the theatre wings.)

The man who sweeps up in the morning doesn't look very cheerful. But how I envy him. At least he can go and have a drink now and then.

Vital capacity test. Urging me to make a good per-formance, the nurse on duty—who deserves to be pitied—yells loudly enough to shatter all the walls of the capital: 'MoreMoreMoreMore . . .' I'd laugh at this if my mouth weren't closed around the end of a vacuum-cleaner-like tube connected to a big machine that records my respiratory input and output in learned graphs. The precautions being taken!

I meet my neighbours. A few *habitués* of the hospital. Members of the old brigade. Nurses' clowns. Regular customers here for the third or fourth time. They've made themselves at home. They smoke in the john, but nobody's duped. Desiring neither to live nor to die. Standing on an abandoned railway-station plat-form. In a church that's lost both its priest and the Good Lord. Dark laughing bursts out.

I'm summoned 'downstairs'. Here I am, sitting on a bench in a corridor, among people wearing street clothes—future companions?—and waiting for their own appointment. They're visitors. I'm wearing pyjamas. As if I were at home. They're afraid. Not me. It's all over. (This reminds me of what Tristan Bernard said when the Nazis came to take him and his wife away.)*

The first question: Wine? Tobacco? Quite a lot of both, sir!

A girl—seventeen or eighteen years old, but will I dare to look longer?—has been working here for only a short while. She has to learn the nurse's trade, get it into the blood, literally. So she has been given a new guinea pig with raw flesh—yours truly—for some kind of special blood test, if I have understood correctly. I hold out my arm as if it were having an erection from my shoulder blade. She misses the vein. She begins again. My arm swells. So the doctor helping her—the nurse is really very pretty, I've now sneaked a look—takes over and, hey, heads for a spot near my balls! My Jesus pops up, uncovered. The doctor, whose number I'd like to jot down, asks the girl to hold my legs. As if I were going to fly off. He sticks the needle deep into my crotch. Misses his mark. Misses again. A second time. The bastard. Either kill him or die. Neither happens. Gallons of sweat. You can get dressed again.

No man-to-man talk. You're no longer a man. Not a 'fellow man'. But, rather, under a decree stripping you of your identity, as if Customs officers had seized all your papers. And when they condescend to relate with you, an obsequiousness for the half-witted or some big backroom joking. It's good to laugh a bit. For your morale—that word for concierges asking how you're doing. But we can't be salvaged. No one could give a damn about what we are, were or—so we hope!—will be. The body, first and foremost. Nothing but the body. That big bloody factory, your guts—that's their business. From a certain viewpoint, what could be more desirable? I've always daydreamt a little of being in this state. But hey, bright boy— only when you'd freely chosen to be in it! And all these questions they ask, with your answers listened to, jotted down—for death's archives, perhaps? What a file! An utterly predictable tale tied up neatly with black ribbons! But you have to be useful to the human race. To its perpetuation. Human beings will come after us. 'That's surprising,' observed Valéry.*

Shots, blood tests, IV drips. A nurse from a poor outlying district is in a bad mood this morning: 'Dammit! What a fuckin' job!' She has come to stick me. She misses me once, twice, three times. 'Where the hell are this guy's veins?' She calls out to another nurse: 'Hey, you take care of him. I'm fed up! Shit on this!' It's a hard job, that's for sure. Perhaps we'll meet again elsewhere.

This morning, a long undershirt open down the back is brought to me. I'm naked underneath. At ten o'clock, a smiling black fellow and his little table on wheels. Your turn, sir. Off we go. The lift. The corridors. The operating theatre . . . That's a fine name to meditate on . . . and medicate! Pleasantries exchanged with the crack of the crack surgeons who's skimpy about washing his hands. I wonder if I'm perhaps pronouncing the last words I'll ever utter . . .

I awake. Where am I? Time has toppled over. I feel alive, touch myself with my fingertips. I'm still here, still here. A small bottle to each side, near my thighs. My neck held tight, as if in cement, especially the left side. A feeding tube up my nose—I know, it's for food, I've seen them. I must look idiotic.

I'm wheeled back into my room. T. comes to visit. In the corridor, the mere sight of me makes her burst out weeping. I console her. Not dead, not dead—there's worse! Then the parade of speaking people. I write on a magic slate. What a laugh. Everyone is delighted I'm taking the situation so well. I'm taking nothing at all. Unless I kill myself. That would be rather stupid. So why not be merry? This is what I'd already thought *before*. So let's be merry!

I get up. It's difficult to put one foot in front of the other. Awfully groggy, all the same. I'm going to tour the corridor. I find my neighbours, we watch what's going on in our midst, what's going on in the street. It's a street I know well. It reminds me of friends: Michel, Roland ... When I was living in Meudon, I would drive up this street, my arse on my motorcycle. We watch. The other people outside. People walking, smoking, speaking and looking sad. We watch. We watch one another. It's a lifestyle.

My roommate isn't doing well. Monsieur Gros. From Clermont-Ferrand. Eighty-three years old. He's had a dreadful blow. Suffocates every night. I insufflate oxygen into his lungs with the help of this big bottle with a pedal ... His eyes show how grateful he is. (He died the day after I left.) At five in the morning, a haughty nurse, perhaps still half-drowsy, arrives to wash out our tracheotomy tubes. The conversation is not very lively, to say the least. The impression of being a dog. Black women are especially fearsome here. Merciless when on the job. Don't cross swords with them. They act like racists in reverse. Obviously, we are no longer human beings for them.

Sheets of saliva. My kingdom (!) for a glass of water.*

It is as if all these people coming to see me are appearing on a screen, on the other side of a pane of glass. They chat with one another, some of them meeting up again after many years—hey, come and have dinner one of these days. They chat. What they're saying isn't any more interesting than usual. But their voices fascinate me. Live voices.

. . . words rise to my lips
yet can't break through the hemmed rim
while my ever-trembling lips
made to be closely observed
burn out any eye watching them
what's he saying we can't hear him
only their looks throw money down
on the table of our face to face . . .

Shots, blood tests, IV drips. There's talk of sending me to Marseille for speech therapy. *Qu'est-ce que c'est?**

This is going to happen. But no openings for the time being. I'll have to wait. Three weeks. IV drips once again, every morning. But there's no more room in my arms. I'm the despair of nurses. They attack my hands. This hospital is only a hundred yards from where I was born.

Every day, the tracheotomy-tube ritual. It has to be washed out carefully. For someone who's never liked to linger in bathrooms, I now act like a woman pampering herself. But it hurts when I slide the tube back into the hole to the left of my glottis. On my last day in the hospital, the interns put the tube in the wrong way. I told them so (as it were!). It doesn't matter. Now the hole bleeds. The crack of the crack surgeons decides to remove the tube. The hole is completely uncovered. Which puts T. into a flutter, for she fears it will shrink, and then . . . The gentlemen burst out laughing.

With my collar, I look like a Protestant minister.

From my window in the Batignolles quarter, I can see Mallarmé's windows on the other side of the railway tracks.* Receive a few good visits. But no way of opening my mouth any more. Writing has become necessary. Which might end up disgusting me with writing. We'll see.

Marseille. A taxi takes T. and me to Château-Gombert where I can perhaps pick up a second-hand voice.* Slightly more than a hundred patients who have been laryngectomized—what a strange word. Thus my kin and kind. The same hunched-over look. That odd something setting us apart. No, not sadness. Rather like an animal that has been tortured, mutilated. Yet that keeps putting up a fight.

An old piano in the physical therapy room. I go there alone after the classes(?) and tap away on it for a while. A very tinny piano, but this matters little. When I stand up to leave, what a surprise to see fifteen of my companions sitting there behind me. They've remained silent, obviously, but there are several sorts of silence. My astonishment at finding them there. The sensation of being in a jungle, a tiger among fellow tigers at the peaceful hour. They give me a modest sign of thanks. You're welcome. To weep. But everything makes you weep. Achtung!

Some good visits. From Nice. From Tunis.

Everyday except Saturday and Sunday, a cobalt session on the other side of town, near Notre-Dame de la Garde with its monumental gilded statue. The ride across town in the ambulance is atrocious, for the driver keeps Radio Monte Carlo blasting away. A desire to commit a murder. What unthinkable bull-shit! Poor Georges de Caunes!* Kill him! Is it really the right moment? Lying beneath the enormous radiation therapy machine, I discover that my mouth is just at the height of the genital organs of the charming woman who is positioning me.

Every day, as soon as we arrive and cross the thresh-old, we come across a new dead person. His dear ones, in the shadows.

The cobalt has begun to burn. My neck is bleeding. A ton of ointment. No way I can swallow. They must be grinding my flesh. Mashing it. Difficult nights spent sitting up, as if in a carriage heading for that other night, the black night. Who knows?

I dwell inside my shadow.

My horror—again confirmed—of this climate, this town, this southern French accent. Even birds get on my nerves, as if they too were chirping with an accent, the poor little creatures. Sitting at the table, you have to bear the songs—that make you want to kill yourself—chortled out by waitresses who think they're entertaining us. Not all of us, not all of us. It's unbelievable, but I've already been in this town before, twice, to act out a comedy! I once set sail for Egypt from here.* What's the connection between the Marseille that I'm now crossing like a sleepwalker, going as far as Vallon des Auffes where I once fell in love, and all the way to the Prado, to the stadium— hey, Skoblar!*—and the man who was rambling about the town . . . some hundred years ago? I no longer know him. I recognize him.

Ah, these girls, or women, in charge of me for the speech therapy sessions! They hand me plays by Molière I know by heart so I can read them aloud, 'burp' them. How cheerful! I disappoint them. Not much sound can be drawn out of me. And yet I don't look all that stupid. But I can't even burp decently, frankly—which is essential. I'm not the only one. A string bean of a fellow keeps me company, in our helplessness. He's been around for a long time—a crippled leg, perhaps from the First World War, he's

been around a long time. He opens his mouth des-
perately. Nothing comes out. We chuckle and get
acquainted. He's the guardian of the Seaside Ceme-
tery at Sète. It's time for us to quote lines from
Valéry's poem. He jots down a few passages from
the said 'Seaside Cemetery'* for me, and I mime
them. We make a good pair. 'The wind rises . . .'*
But you should hear us every morning as we try to
burp out sounds, the young women chatting away
in the corner. A true concert of sea lions, of moles
with stuffy noses. Some patients jump the gun and
burp away with childish delight. They're the ones
who'll be reintegrated into society. I have no talent.
The young women retort—you aren't motivated! A
few veteran patients pay us a visit. As models to
follow. They spread the good word. You see, every-
thing is back to normal. This oesophageal speech
works perfectly well . . . In desperation, others have
opted for a sort of microphone they hold against a
part of their neck. A noise worse than death comes
out, if ever . . . No, not that.

A little respite at the thought of Rimbaud croaking
not very far from here. And of Artaud, born nearby
. . . Well then, I might as well croak here too!

I ask to leave before the end. The cobalt sessions are over. Never mind the speech therapy which had got off to a bad start, anyway. After all, enough said. It's your turn, my brothers!

Cured more of life than death.

I'm no longer afraid of dying. As if it's already happened. Good riddance. (Alas!)

I've been thrown off kilter with respect to what made my stability possible, my walk-on role acceptable, between yelling—henceforth soundless—and giving up. I'm standing alongside a former ego who's loved, experienced, *something else*.

Standing up in the Marseille–Paris train, in the vestibule between two crowded cars. This is the first time I've found myself alone in society with my new status. I've even been given a card to show if I run into difficulty. Give me mouth-to-neck respiration . . . But I'm unaccustomed to this. In the Paris bus taking me to the Montparnasse train station, people get angry because my enormous sack blocks part of the exit door. I catch myself talking back no less sharply but my mouth remains open like a bird with the pip disease. Nothing comes out. I'll have to be careful not to get upset, not to play the bad-tempered little runt. But how *idiotic* I must suddenly look . . .

The Paris–Quimper night train. What remains happy inside me? A taxi ride all the way to Dz. Not expecting me, Tania is already up. Tears. But the kids react well. No uncalled-for fatherliness from them, no pity of the 'my poor lil Daddy' kind. That would have been atrocious. A good situation to take advantage of. All I need to do now is play the clown, moderately. Modestly. A silent film. I used to like doing mime, when I could speak. People would say—stop acting stupid! This is where we're at now.

In the street. Those who cross to the other pavement so they won't have to say hello. Do I have the plague? Cancer isn't contagious.

Surgeons. They manage to behave in such a way that life is not at stake but, rather, death. They're more concerned about conquering death—a little—than about making life last—a little—longer. This changes all the relationships.

All these tobacco pipes bear witness to a human presence. And so does their odour, probably, but I can't smell anything any more. A man has lived here, dreaming, smoking, writing. The tobacco box is full. Like moss on the floor—splotches of grey tobacco. Where is this man? I know he's not dead. Simply disabled, *diminished*. I know that he was operated on alive because of something other than poetry—no anaesthesia is needed for that. That he's lost his voice. That he'll likely die without it. With that hole through which he coughs, spits, *breathes*. You don't get used to it right away. It needs to be hidden from everyone. Apparently it can make them faint. For that, there are protections that give you a false—a true—clergyman's appearance. What you make out inside is dark, disturbing, with the Minotaur lurking . . .

To resuscitate without being dead.

I now have too many reasons—don't toss out any more on the table—to be as I already was: in 'good health.' I'm not disgusted but, rather, in a state of having come back from somewhere and seen . . . Actually, more of having seen nothing at all than of having seen it all before. Here I am—a revenant. A final promotion?

The local doctors who had treated us for various trifles, with whom I had made light conversation wherever I ran into them—the street, the football stadium—avoid me. As if I'd betrayed them. Cancer is too much for them. A sort of capitalism. (Indeed the only capitalism that makes them run away.) Out of their depth. Offended. And I myself can no longer imagine needing them for anything. What in fact am I going to die of?

The difference between the warrior's silence and the sick man's silence.

Guys whom I haven't seen for years—we had stopped writing letters to one another—now send me messages of friendship. No, they haven't forgotten me. (As for me, I'd forgotten them.) They even declare that I'm a great fellow. And so I am! Such is cancer.

It's true there's comedy in tragedy, as long as . . . let's not exaggerate. Yet here I am with a front-row seat. Those pains in the neck who would stop and tell me all about one of their lives, and who now complain I won't be able to talk to them any more . . .

Odd to have death—your own!—no longer in front of you but, rather, to have the impression that it's behind you. That you've passed it by, thumbing your nose at it in the rear-view mirror. It's Jabès who wrote: 'How could one be dead and live until one's death?'* Well, this must be possible.

I must have treated myself as I did my motorcycles. Till they couldn't take any more, and not bothering much about maintenance. Why does this hole in my neck make me think of the one in which a sparkplug fits? And the way I would bleed, of leaking oil?

We're advised to keep a whistle. In case we fall into a hole.

Who lets us write when we are in good health?

What's essential—changing gears. As if passing from west to east.

They can't cure you. They postpone.

I'm in their midst. I'm spoken of in the third person, as if I were retarded: 'He looks well.'

Why does one pay a visit to a sick person? But there are also those who never miss a funeral. Here, for example, quite a few holier-than-thou old biddies read the obituaries every day—let's go, it's your turn! You amuse yourself however you can.

After all, silence is another language. One that everyone knows. But we're ashamed to use a skill that can't be learnt.

It's incredible how many people I knew, invited into my home, who never spoke at all. At the dinner table or while taking a walk, you had to keep the conversation going. And wasn't it rather the dull or wild looks in their eyes while I was spieling off more or less coherently, remaining more or less at their service, even at their level—you don't understand anything of what others say when they go to a little trouble and don't look down on you—that slyly ended up slipping me this slyest of illnesses—no pain, no warning—this cancer? As if their nasty, evil silence—sometimes accompanied by the grim excuse that I knew how to express myself—had drop by drop infiltrated like a poison through the walls of my throat. Oh, I'm not making anything up! It seems to me I already knew.

Everybody is so persuaded that everybody else cheats—as if it were possible!—it suffices to have a cancer in order to get everybody to absolve you—at last, a man who doesn't cheat.

Mouth. A room, a cave, a space reverberating with the echoes of a monstrous blabber, an orgy of words. A deserted dance hall, as after a ball. I chew confetti. What are words if they aren't masks hiding only themselves? Ad infinitum.

One of the horrors of this world—happiness is possible only for poor people who want to remain so. Who'd go out and get themselves killed in order to stay so.

Before, I was sure I was going to die. Now I no longer know. Somewhat left by the wayside. Less interesting. As if death had somehow neglected to pick up what already has . . . a hole in it. Is disabled. I no longer weigh in as heavily as expected. Death won't get all of me.

All he lacks is speech.

The accursed prestige of cancer. I don't have to show off. It's a word I liked neither to utter nor to write. But poetry is merely this same fear, inverted. Every word has its dangers.

Now I'm the citizen of a country whose language is universal. But what's noisier than a jungle?

New routines—pacing up and down. Not a hundred, but ten steps back and forth, for hours on end. Why did I weep when I left the hospital? We're strangely made.

At the edge of mankind as if at the edge of the sea. I hear the noise of their words, as if they were waves. But I can't take a dip any more.

This kind of consideration from afar is strange. For there's no merit, nor any special curse, in having a cancer. It's as if others were grateful to you for having one and for not getting into a sick state about it. But it's not a sickness.

I no longer speak. So nobody speaks to me any more. They speak about me in front of me. And when someone is alone with me, he can't wait to head out of the door. This is perfectly understandable. I can't make anyone feel interesting any more—a hard job that I know how to do well. He pulls his ears down over his eyes. 'How sad it is . . .'

It's nonetheless true that psychology, or a sense of restraint, is used by the privileged classes as an excuse. Not to mention eroticism, that luxury of all luxuries. The Marquis de Sade spent a great part of his life in prison. But he sired some small children. Not to mention Christ. Some very small children.

Soon I'll have forgotten—and I won't be the only one—that I was also one of those abnormal people who speak—crosswise. Across what?

When I'm with others these days, a sort of light haze or mist quickly arises—suitable for the occasion—that at once draws me near and keeps me at a distance from them. Before, I would put on my raincoat or take off all my clothes—and dive right into the conversation. For better or worse, I'd wade through the other's words. (I've never been able to float on my back. Forbidden.) All told, it was rather gruelling. The other person would let you do all the work once he'd sensed you were in a state of 'goodwill'. But ever since I no longer have to speak, the very duration of communication has changed. Has changed gears. I'm no longer given the time to respond. My only concern is with the back of the other's words. A big broad back.

Before: 'The most important thing is to be in good health . . .'

Now: 'The most important thing is to keep up your morale . . .'

What you have to listen to!

I can't do anything any more for the solitude of other people. This is less an ordeal than a confirmation.

Speech. They always talk to me about something else.

It's odd to know and sense you're irredeemable. With women, for example. They look at you as if they were glancing emptily at an object in a paltry shop window. Oh, this is better than pity!

I meet up with my mother on the street. We've never had much to say to each other. 'So you've nothing to tell me?' she asks. I make a slightly desperate face. But also apparently a comical one for she holds back her laughter which, unrestrained, would have been perfect. I kiss her forehead. She manages to mutter a bird-like hello. Instead of watching my lips in order to make out my words—this actually works, my twelve-year-old daughter understands everything I say—my mother stands *sideways* and simply utters, atrociously, 'yes' or 'no' in an unrelated fashion. Briefly stated, nothing has changed. Let's continue our stroll.

A theatrical distancing effect. Play the role of a guy stricken with cancer and catch the disease; become he who's playing the role.

An advancing tide of dead people. My dead people. My lovers, my friends, all of them for ever speechless. No, this is no consolation.

Nor what I'd noticed before—that gestures suffice for almost everything.

After all, the pleasure of living remains. That's not too bad.

Disease puts health to shame. Health doesn't know which way to turn (and I'm being polite) in order to become interesting, to become ill, but at the right moment. Who doesn't catch his little neurosis?

Odd (for the second or third time!) to think that I'd *surely* already be dead if I'd not undergone surgery. Starting with this idea, how to live more fully? To take advantage of life? I try. I tell myself: 'Hey old guy, it's great to be here still, with your loved ones, with Nature, that old maid with her eternal menstrual cycles!' Self-persuasion. But I do slacken my pace, 'verify' better.

The saw—there's worse. Dreamt I was a legless cripple. Relieved when I awoke and counted my limbs.

Being speechless simply lets an interval of time—which is often nasty, harmful—flow by, flow away, whereas speaking slowed it down, kept it from settling in, from feeling at home. The time to be someone.

What's goodness? This is the last question left that still might interest me. I'm not yet out of the woods!

The ideal companion for a speechless man—a deaf woman. I was once quite close to loving one—and to getting myself loved by her. A Russian woman. I was destined for Russia, a country which, moreover, has something deaf about it.* In all the senses of the word. Snow-clad. Uncompromising.

The smell of flowers, seaweed, the ocean . . . My sense of smell is gone. Apparently it comes back. Ten or twenty per cent of it.

Advice for the speechless: Go and live in a country in which you don't know the language. They'll be less surprised at your own.

Whatever I'm doing, I'm constantly stopped short—and catch myself in such a state—by my astonishment at still being here, as if I'd packed my suitcase and then received a countermand. But perhaps I'm exaggerating. Imagining things. And I unwillingly imagine horrible things. For example, at the kitchen table, surrounded by my wife and kids, by dog and cat: 'If I were not here, what would that matter?'

The impression of having been beheaded. And then that my head was put back on, yet a little sideways. Our *shifted* look . . .

Physicians and surgeons have special knowledge. But it's wrong to think this knowledge makes them 'better' or 'more human', enabling them to transcend the simple limits of their job. What job, in fact, enables that? It's nonetheless a fact that they 'constipate' us, fascinate us. Whose fault is it? Isn't it shameful to make us mumble Corneille, Racine and the like instead of introducing us quickly to the bloody darkness of our bodies? We dimwits would look a bit wittier—how's that for punning poetry!—whenever we happened to fart the wrong way. And perhaps those *Science* gentlemen, all of a sudden, would be less unpleasant.

Life, a thin layer. It's likely you'll give up on yourself. Go senile. Give up. It's more difficult to content yourself with the energy necessary for maintaining an upright position. To *let yourself go*, an act that's not possible for everyone. What remains intact in us? For death? What's redistributed in man because it doesn't die at the same time as the man?

Tania: 'Why you?' Superstition. As if I'd been pun-
ished, after hiding something from her. No, not at
all!

Believing in God means fearing the judgement of
human beings.

'Those who know do not speak;
those who speak do not know.
Block the passages,
Shut the doors,
Let all sharpness be blunted,
All tangles untied,
All glare tempered,
All dust smoothed.
This is called the mysterious levelling.
He who has achieved it cannot either be drawn into
friendship or repelled,
Cannot be benefited, cannot be harmed,
Cannot either be raised or humbled,
And for that very reason is highest of all creatures
under heaven.'*

Tao-te-Ching

Bravo! Only one obstacle—the affections. What a
bony snag! A skeleton!

Softening of the tissues. I should've stopped drinking, smoking. Indeed. Why? I'd be rather inclined (!) to believe that cancer, in any case my cancer, comes from this. Abuse. Negligence. Nicotine trickled from my pipes; tar often left its blackness on my tongue. This fine deposit must have trickled—kept slowly trickling—into my throat—and that's why your girl can't speak! And then, let's be honest—a little . . . existential weariness, a little fed up with being a human being instead of something else in such a world. Hence an attack by the enemy, by the illness, on abandoned, undefended ground. When an illness isn't hereditary, it develops on friendly ground. You want to die and don't want to die. You make last what no longer has any amorous future, in general or specifically—and what other future would you like to have? You take care of, you stuff, this body that our own dear free will pushes to its own loss in order to make us into something. As if death needed the body's services. Vain solidarity.

The choice. Reintegrate into society. Why do so? There's only one problem—the wife and kids who live with me. Who must put up with me. I think this matter has been taken care of. For the best in the worst of cases. As to what remains—*exchanges*, people—my ledger was full, thank you. I had students.

Yes, this is the only truly painful thorn. But they will manage just fine without me. I've had my noseful of the *smug* speech of people nowadays—if I may once again evoke that poor organ. We're less and less funny. This is not quite the right word, but it gives you an idea. An Amazonian Indian surely possesses more that can move, set in motion my words than my neighbours, taken at large all around. Who live in the same period as I do. A sad age. If I recount what happens to me on a given day, I perceive that speaking is completely superfluous. I've suffered a lot, but I have especially suffered from speaking, from having to speak, to indifferent people who are standing upright yet are dead or are dead yet sitting down. To bastards as well, who would *watch* me unwinding and would count the stitches, or the knitting stitches that they would themselves unravel. Foreigners with the same tongue as mine. With whom it's possible not to understand one another. Friendship also exists; this is true and I don't turn my nose up at it. Yet in the final reckoning, I'm fifty-four years old; nearly all the people I loved, who loved me (why not?), have died. Yes, a choice must be made. What's the use of making an appearance again, of learning how to speak again with this voice from beyond the grave, which has lost all resonance, this voice of the dead man I drag along on borrowed time? Everything I listen to—on the radio, on television—disgusts me. I never intended to get myself elected to parliament. I'm only a witness to an enormous abuse of dead speech, atrociously painted up, an ageing belle, all swollen with bruises, pedantic, opinionated, with everyone slicing into it in order to participate in a possessive degradation— pathetically small parts of a mouldy cake which are aristocratically sampled nevertheless. Enough's enough, shit on it all! As long as manuscripts keep getting sent to me—after all, that's my job—then my new state of being changes nothing in that regard. We'll manage to get by.

Speaking, *keeping the conversation going*, caring about the kind of verbal gaiety that blocks off incessant chat about the latest film, the latest book, amidst all the idleness of social life, my dear, etc., in other words, attentive not to let boredom crack the potential pleasure of being together—I'm never bored when I'm alone—this was one of my passions, one of my vices, with a few other, rather common ones: hitting the road, tobacco, motorcycles, women, all of these passions unappeased, edgy, ever ready to be put back on the grill of impatience. The *erotic* side of communication, beyond all superior Platonism. How many people delight in perpetuating the reputation of being 'dark, brooding, good-looking' types. 'He never says anything. He always seems elsewhere, etc.' None of that for me. I hated not chipping in with my two bits, and I'd avoid all intellectual allusions, starting up a conversation immediately in the very heart of a cultureless zone without memories, and this enabled me to hang out wholeheartedly with all the human races, intellectuals as well as sea fishermen, travelling companions for whom I was willingly a total stranger to their specific occupations, even as I required them to remain strangers to mine in this quest for the most basic forms of encounter, conversation and pleasure. Women conceal their sexual organs; men, their speech. Their words are buried, lost, distraught. I'll have spent a great part of my life (the greatest part) attempting to draw out the unique tone of their voices, rummaging through their private syntax which lies at the farthest remove possible from the one making relationships possible in a time quickly recovered by politics, bookishness, trivial anecdotes. An amorous syntax needing a wide field staked out for it so it can unfold (and be reassured). The musical score doesn't exist—you improvise as you play. A hesitant syntax. This is how two men engaged in a conversation come closer together, get lost, try each other out, one word opening the way to the next, in the unending twilight of the forest of raw language. (Cf. the echo of Weber's 'Wolf's Glen'.)* I'll have adored this peaceful hunt (my friends won't say the contrary) until I'm full, until the closing of the doors, the turning off of the lights.

The line—garlic of memory!—that comes to mind most often: 'When our heart has made its harvest once . . .'*

March 1976–March 1977

NOTES

P. 6 | *'The best definition of man is found in La Fontaine'*
The French poet and fabulist Jean de La Fontaine (1621–95) wrote these lines in the preface to *Les Amours de Psyché et de Cupidon* (1669), a novel written in both verse and prose.

P. 9 | *'. . . this "nevermore" chills me with horror.'* Perros uses the English word 'nevermore', which is known to the French because of Charles Baudelaire's (1821–67) and Stéphane Mallarmé's (1842–98) admiration for and translations of Edgar Allan Poe (1809–49). In Perros' day, Julien Gracq (1910–2007) and others continued to underscore the importance of Poe.

P. 11 | *'Had Napoleon been able to become Chateaubriand . . .'*
The French emperor Napoleon Bonaparte (1769–1821) and the writer François René de Chateaubriand (1768–1848) entertained a long, complex and turbulent political relationship.

P. 12 | *'"Thus when I sucked the clarity of grapes . . ."'* The line is by Mallarmé, 'L'Après-midi d'un faune' (1876).

P. 14 | *'The mote is literature. The beam is you, reading.'* An allusion to Matthew 7:3: 'And why beholdest thou the mote that is in thy brother's eye, but considerest not the beam that is in thine own eye?'

P. 15 | '. . . *that Javert in pursuit of a wretched man . . .*'
Javert is the police inspector in Victor Hugo's *Les
Misérables* (1862). He commits suicide when he real-
izes that Jean Valjean, whom he has been trying to
arrest, is a good man.

P. 18 | '*Debussy wrote all his music while sitting in an aquar-
ium.*' The French composer Claude Debussy (1862–
1918) composed numerous piano pieces evoking
water or fish.

P. 25 | '"*If God does not exist, everything is permitted.*"'
Fyodor Dostoevsky, *The Brothers Karamazov* (1880).

P. 27 | '*Don Juan is the man . . .*' Perros is probably thinking
of Molière's play, *Dom Juan ou le festin de Pierre*, first
staged in 1665. But the proverbial lover appears in
the work of many other writers, playwrights and
poets.

P. 28 | '*Making mistakes in English . . .*' I have transformed
Perros' remark about French grammar into a remark
about English. The French original evokes the
malapropism *ennuyant* (as opposed to the correct
ennuyeux).

P. 29 | '*Love needs to be reinvented.*' From Rimbaud's prose
text 'Delirium I "The Foolish Virgin"' (*A Season in
Hell*, 1873): 'He will say: "I don't love women. Love
needs to be reinvented, it's obvious. Women are no

longer capable of wanting anything but a secure life. Once that's achieved, feeling and beauty are forgotten: all that's left is cold disdain, the very stuff that marriage feeds on nowadays. Or else I come across women who have signs of happiness about them, with whom I could have had close companionship, and there they are, devoured from the outset by brutes who are about as sensitive as a pile of logs ..."' (translated by Mark Treharne, *A Season in Hell: And Illuminations*, London: Dent, 1998).

P. 31 | '*See Heidegger.*' *Paper Collage* reveals that Perros was a reader of the German philosopher Martin Heidegger (1889–1976), whose writings were much discussed at the time in regard to French poets, especially René Char (1907–88).

PAPER COLLAGE 2

P. 42 | '*Renard, indeed, because of his sharp vision ...*' Perros puns here with the name of the writer and playwright Jules Renard (1864–1910). 'Renard' literally means 'fox', and the poet is perhaps also thinking of the mediaeval tales collected in *Le Roman de Renart*. In French, Julius Caesar is Jules César. The play *Le Plaisir de rompre* dates to 1897.

P. 44 | '*It's a sport, a kind of exercise, in Valéry's sense of the term.*' Paul Valéry wrote daily, from 1894 to his death in 1945, in a series of 261 notebooks. He originally did not wish to publish these *Cahiers*, considering them to collect only his 'mental exercise'.

P. 46 | '*All the words are in the dictionary.*' Comte de Lautréamont (1846–70) is famous for the poems collected in *Chants de Maldoror*, beloved by the Surrealists. Mallarmé's long poem, 'Un coup de dés n'abolira jamais le hazard' appeared in 1897, the year before he died. The German poet Friedrich Hölderlin (1770–1843) began using the pen name Scardanelli in 1841, two years before he died. The reference to Antonin Artaud (1896–1948) alludes to his writings before, and after, his confinements in various mental asylums in and around Paris, and then in Rodez (where he underwent as many as fifty-eight electroshock treatment sessions), during the last eleven years of his life.

P. 48 | '*There's spontaneity in the surging forth of a source.*' Perros perhaps remotely refers to the well-known line 'an enigma is something that surges forth purely' ('Ein Rätsel ist Reinentsprungenes'), found in the fourth strophe of Hölderlin's 'The Rhine' (1801).

P. 51 | '*Make yourself into that Other evoked by Rimbaud . . .*' The famous remark 'Je est un autre' (I am an Other), which the poet made in his letter to Paul Demeny on 15 May 1871.

P. 53 | *'Valéry claimed the first line comes from the gods.'* Perros alludes to Valéry's oft-quoted remark in *Au sujet d'Adonis* (1920): 'The Gods graciously give us, *for nothing*, such and such a first line; but it's up to us to fashion the second line, which must harmonize with the other one and not be unworthy of its supernatural elder brother.'

P. 56 | *'"In the deserted East . . ."'* A line from the play *Bérénice* (1670) by Jean Racine (1639–99). French readers know the entire line: *'Dans l'Orient désert quel devint mon ennui!'* (In the deserted East, what my weariness became).

P. 63 | *'So I waited until my words lined up like Panurge's sheep . . .'* Perros refers to a scene in Rabelais's *Pantagruel* (1532). Panurge buys a sheep. Thinking that he has been done in by the merchant, he throws the sheep into the sea. But the other sheep in the herd follow the first over the side of the boat. The French expression refers to someone who follows others regardless of the consequences.

'What makes Mallarmé a poet different from others . . .' At the end, the reference to Mallarmé's 'tombeaux' or

funeral tributes include those to his son Anatole, and Baudelaire, Verlaine and Poe.

P. 64 | '*Anatole's death comes at the right* grave *moment.*' The death of Anatole Mallarmé (1871–79) inspired his father to take some two hundred pages of notes in the hopes of writing a *Tombeau d'Anatole.* The poem was left unfinished but is often studied as an especially important aspect of Mallarmé's poetry (and of poetic modernism). The poem and notes were edited by the critic Jean-Pierre Richard and published by Éditions du Seuil in 1961.

P. 65 | '. . . *when Gide received me at his home, rue Vaneau.*' According to the biographical notes accompanying the poetry collection *Une vie ordinaire*, Perros would have visited André Gide (1869–1951) at some point during the years 1942–44. Thierry Gillyboeuf has pointed out to me that Gide's letter of 8 July 1945 to Perros suggests that the visit might rather have taken place in 1945. See also the passage in Guillyboeuf's biography, *Georges Perros* (Éditions La Part Commune, 2003, pp. 32–3). Many French writers have left remembrances of being received by Gide, not only a famous novelist but also an influential editor at Gallimard.

P. 67 | '. . . *I told him that the wait was over, that I had lost my virginity in a review,*' Gillyboeuf (*Georges Perros,* pp. 61–3) recounts Perros' first publication—a series of 'notes' published by Paulhan in the *Nouvelle Nouvelle Revue Française* (1 August 1953). Following up on Paulhan's suggestion, Georges Poulot took on the pen name 'Georges Perros' so he would not be confused with the Belgian critic and philosopher Georges Poulot (1902–91). Under his real name, Perros had published a few brief pieces in *La Dictature Lettriste*, the first magazine published by the Lettriste movement.

P. 69 | *'Behind closed yeses.'* By writing 'Le Oui-clos', Perros plays with the French *huis-clos*, the legal term for 'in camera' or 'behind closed doors', and thus also with the title of Jean-Paul Sartre's play *Huis clos* (1943).

P. 71 | *'Woman is the body of man.'* Perros perhaps parodies a well-known line by the poet Louis Aragon (1897– 1982): 'L'avenir de l'homme, c'est la femme'—'The future of man is woman' (*Le Fou d'Elsa*, 1963). In daily usage, the quotation is often inverted: 'La femme, c'est l'avenir de l'homme' (Woman is the future of man).

'Vive la frousse. La Frouce.' The French original con- cludes with this untranslatable pun, which suggests an official ceremony, even a military commemoration, at which one would say 'Vive la France'. *Frousse* is a slang for 'fear' and the homophonous *Frouce* makes one think of 'France'. One could transform Perros' quip about France into a remark about the United States, for example, 'God bless the United Scaredy Cats of America'.

P. 73 | *'Einstein saying: If I could live my life over again, I'd be a plumber.'* Something must have been lost in translation when Perros first read this statement, for the original has a different focus: 'If I would be a young man again and had to decide how to make my living, I would not try to become a scientist or scholar or teacher. I would rather choose to be a plumber or a peddler in the hope to find that modest degree of independence still available under present circumstances' (*The Reporter*, 13 October 1954).

P. 74 | *'Gide believed in God through his wife.'* The Catholic beliefs of Gide's wife Madeleine are well known, as are the writer's own grappling with his Protestant family background.

P. 76 | *'"The being of literature is nothing but its technique."'* This quotation became well known in French because of Roland Barthes's essay 'La Réponse de Kafka' (*Essais critiques*, 1964), an article that was first published in 1960. Barthes traces the analysis back to the critic Marthe Robert (*Kafka*, Gallimard, 1960).

PAPER COLLAGE 3

P. 79 | '. . . *a sort of Grévin Wax Museum . . .*' The famous wax museum located in Montmartre.

P. 85 | '. . . *the shadow of a man on a Hiroshima pavement.*' Perros refers to John Hersey's pioneering article, 'Hiroshima', which first appeared in the *New Yorker* (31 August 1946).

P. 95 | '*Another person is like a distant province.*' Perros' 'La province, c'est l'autre' includes a remote echo of Sartre's 'L'Enfer, c'est les autres' (*Huis clos*). Perros' quip can thus be interpreted in various ways.

P. 97 | '*We all die young.*' Perros is probably thinking of the classical expression 'He whom the Gods love dies young.' The expression comes from the mythical story of Trophonius and Agamedes, two brothers who built Apollo's temple at Delphi. As related in the *Homeric Hymns to Apollo*, the oracle informed the brothers that, once they had finished their work, they could do anything they wanted for six days; on the seventh day their greatest wish would be fulfilled. They were found dead. Variants of the expression appear in plays by Menander, Plautus and others.

P. 103 | '. . . *Saint-Malo—a perfectly sinister town, probably because of its inhabitants.*' Perros is being ironic here because this port on the northern coast of Brittany attracts many tourists. The town is famous for its high stone ramparts and historical centre, much of which was in fact completely reconstructed after the bombings of the Second World War.

P. 105 | *'During his Ethiopian years . . .'* Rimbaud's 'Ethiopian years' refer to the last period of the French poet's life. He had given up writing poetry in about 1875 and, after numerous land trips and sea voyages, he began working in Abyssinia in 1880. Countless French poets and critics have analysed these years when Rimbaud had completely given up writing.

'I think it's Henri de Régnier . . .' Henri de Régnier (1874–1936) was a French writer and poet who was close to Mallarmé's circle. The actual quotation is 'vivre avilit'.

'. . . what Yves Bonnefoy calls the hinterland.' Yves Bonnefoy's (b. 1923) 'hinterland' alludes to his book *L'Arrière-pays* (Skira, 1972), published in English as *The Arrière-Pays* by Seagull Books in 2012.

P. 107 | *'Many politicians are failed writers.'* Much more than in English-speaking countries, there is a long tradition in France of politicians writing books, even novels. No presidential candidate ever begins his campaign without first publishing a book.

'"*A pistol is a little stupid*."' From the posthumously published poem 'Une mort trop travaillée' (1920) by Tristan Corbière (1845–75).

P. 108 | '*Stendhal dreamt of being Molière . . .*' Molière's *Miser* (1668) is one of the French playwright's most famous plays. Stendhal's great novel *The Chartreuse of Parma* was published in 1839.

P. 112 | '"*Monsieur Verdelin's here . . .*"' Perros perhaps recalls a character in Balzac's play *Mercadet le faiseur* (1851).

P. 118 | '*Sartre—a vegetarian who likes only raw meat.*' The French philosopher Jean-Paul Sartre (1905–80) was known for consuming alcohol, barbiturates and any kind of food available (with the notable exception of seafood), but the observation seems to relate to his literary treatment of things, of the raw materials of life.

P. 121 | '*The kid is eating a* Lu *butter biscuit.*' A famous brand of Breton butter biscuits.

'*We're travelling between Redon and Vannes.*' Redon and Vannes are towns in Brittany. The irony here is that the grandfather is reading *Le Monde*, mostly read only by Parisians.

SO TO SPEAK

P. 137 | '*If I is an Other, I speak of the Other when I say I.*' Again, a quotation of Rimbaud's well-known remark from his aforementioned letter to Demeny.

'*If genuine life is absent, I speak of absence when I speak of my life.*' Rimbaud's equally well-known remark, '*la vraie vie est absente*', from the prose text 'Delirium I "The Foolish Virgin"' (*A Season in Hell*).

THE MAGIC SLATE

P. 143 | '*Nothing, it's nothing, not even pharyngitis, a few red spots, no frog to fuss about.*' I am assuming, though it is not entirely clear, that Perros puns with the French expression 'avoir un chat dans la gorge' (literally, 'to have a cat in your throat').

P. 144 | '*Every Thursday, in Brest . . .*' Perros gave what he called an 'ignorance course' at the University of Brest, beginning in 1970. According to Gillyboeuf's biography, Perros was officially supposed to teach diction. Perros' classes took place in the back room of the bar Chez Michou. The biography cites two vivid remembrances of these 'courses'.

'. . . *Tolbiac* . . .' Perros is probably thinking of a quarter located in the thirteenth arrondissement of Paris.

Otherwise, the Battle of Tolbiac, at which the Frankish king Clovis defeated the Alamans, is of course known to the French who learn about the event at school.

'...*Balto*...' Balto (1923–33), the famous dog-sledge husky who transported precious anti-diphtheria serum to the victims of an epidemic in Alaska.

P. 145 | '*A man named L., the crack of the crack surgeons, will perform the operation.*' The surgeon's name was Professor Laccoureye.

P. 147 | '*Jean Richepin, Jehan Rictus and Georges Fourest!*' Jean Richepin (1849–1926) was a French poet and novelist, famous for his *Chansons des gueux* (1876), a series of poems written in the slang of beggars, petty criminals and poor people. Jehan Rictus (1887–1933) was a French poet who wrote verse in colloquial French. Georges Fourest (1867–1945) was a Symbolist poet who parodied the classics.

P. 148 | '*L. Hospital.*' The Hôpital Laennec in the seventh arrondissement of Paris.

P. 151 | '*This reminds me of what Tristan Bernard said...*' Tristan Bernard (1866–1947), the French novelist and playwright, was arrested in Nice during the German Occupation because of his Jewish origins. As he was being taken away, he quipped to his wife:

'Up to now we have lived in anguish. Now we will live in hope.' He was liberated from the Drancy Camp when Sacha Guity and Arletty intervened in his favour.

P. 152 | *'Human beings will come after us. "That's surprising,"* *observed Valéry.'* The remark is found in *Tel quel* (1941). The quotation in French: 'Entendez la parole la plus étrange: *Il y aura des hommes après nous.*'

P. 155 | *'My kingdom* (!) *for a glass of water.'* An allusion to Shakespeare's *Richard III*: 'A horse! a horse! my kingdom for a horse!'

P. 156 | 'Qu'est-ce que c'est?' In the French original, Perros uses English: 'What is this?'

P. 157 | *'From my window in the Batignolles quarter, I can see* *Mallarmé's windows . . .'* After his operation at the Hôpital Laennec, Perros stayed for a few days at the apartment of his wife Tania's son, Patrice. The apartment was located on the rue Boursault, in the seventeenth arrondissement. Mallarmé lived on the rue de Rome, a street that runs parallel to the rue Boursault and that is located just across the railway tracks of the Gare Saint-Lazare. See letter 778 in Perros' *Correspondance 1955–1978* (Gallimard, 1996) with Michel Butor. As Gillyboeuf reports in his biography, the poet was born on the rue Claude-Pouillet, located not far from there.

P. 157 | *'A taxi takes T. and me to Château-Gombert . . .'* The Clinique Château-Gombert still exists.

P. 158 | *'Poor Georges de Caunes!'* Georges de Caunes (1919–2004), well-known radio and television personality.

P. 159 | *'I once set sail for Egypt from here.'* Perros went with the Comédie-Française to Egypt in March 1950. There he met the philosopher Jean Grenier (1898–1971), whose book *Les Îles* (1933) he greatly admired. A long correspondence and a rather difficult friendship between the two men ensued.

'. . .—hey, Skoblar!—. . .' Perros likely refers to Josip Skoblar (b. 1945), an outstanding Yugoslav football player who was on the Marseille team between 1969 and 1975. Perros was an avid sports fan.

P. 160 | *'. . . "Seaside Cemetery". . .'* ('Le Cimetière Marin', 1920), one of Valéry's best-known poems.

'"The wind rises . . ."' A quotation of the first line of the last strophe of Valéry's poem: 'Le vent se lève! . . . Il faut tenter de vivre!' (The wind rises! . . . I need to try to live!).

P. 165 | *'It's Jabès who wrote . . .'* Edmond Jabès (1912–91) was a French poet of Egyptian Jewish origin.

P. 173 | *'A Russian woman. I was destined for Russia . . .'* Perros refers to his subsequent encounter with Tania, a Russian woman whom he meets in 1953 while she is married to a compatriot. She already has two children. Georges and Tania marry in 1963. Three children are born.

P. 175 | ' "*Those who know do not speak . . .*"' The translation of the fifty-sixth chapter of the Tao-te-Ching is by Arthur Waley.

P. 180 | '. . . *Weber's "Wolf's glen"*' A key setting in Carl Maria von Weber's opera *Der Freishutz* (1821).

'. . ."*When our heart has made its harvest once.*"' Baudelaire, 'XL. Semper eadem', *The Flowers of Evil* (1857).